SECRET BARCELONA

Dani Cortijo and Rocío Sierra Carbonell
with the collaboration of Berta de March and Carlos Mesa

ÉDITIONS JONGLEZ

Travel guides

Dani Cortijo - A history graduate from the University of Barcelona (UB), Dani Cortijo specialises in the city's history and is a secondary-school teacher. For years he worked as an Official Catalonian Tourist Guide, focussing on revealing unknown sides of the city to Barcelona locals. In 2009 he won Catalonia's Culture Blog Award for his altresbarcelones.com project, and has spent the past 15 years researching and shedding light on the history of the city through books, TV, radio and the written press. He has had his own sections as a collaborator on a range of media outlets, most prominently Catalunya Ràdio, Betevé and, currently, NacióDigital.

Rocío Sierra Carbonell - Rocío Sierra Carbonell is a freelance journalist and documentary filmaker. Having lived in 5 continents, she now resides in Madrid with her two young kids. These days, Rocio mainly travels in her imagination, writing fiction for tv, theatre, and feature films. After decades of writing about investment, finance, and tourism, she is now immersed in the world of electronic music, and finds herself exploring the fascinating fusion of flamenco-funk-hip-hop.

Berta de March - Barcelonan at heart and by birth, she has lived in several of Barcelona's main neighborhoods, which has allowed her to explore each of them and many more. Translator and editorial collaborator, her contribution to this book has been a challenge to discover even more remote places in her beloved city.

Carlos Mesa - A journalist specialising in new technologies and historical enigmas, Carlos Mesa is currently a contributor on magazines and TV and radio programmes dealing with subjects surrounding journeys and mystery. He has written a number of books, including: *Planeta Insólito* (Pub: Lulu); *Mayan Prophecies: Myth and Reality* (Pub: Nowtilus); *Rennes-le-Château: nuevas revelaciones* (Amazon eBook) and *Gaudí desvelado* (Pub: Dédalo). Carlos is also an official tourist guide offering tours of the unusual side of Barcelona (planetainsolito.es).

We have taken great pleasure in drawing up *Secret Barcelona* and hope that through its guidance you will, like us, continue to discover unusual, hidden or little-known aspects of the city.

Descriptions of certain places are accompanied by thematic sections highlighting historical details or anecdotes as an aid to understanding the city in all its complexity.

Secret Barcelona also draws attention to the multitude of details found in places that we may pass every day without noticing. These are an invitation to look more closely at the urban landscape and, more generally, a means of seeing our own city with the curiosity and attention that we often display while travelling elsewhere ...

Comments on this guidebook and its contents, as well as information on places we may not have mentioned, are more than welcome and will enrich future editions.

Don't hesitate to contact us:
E-mail: info@jonglezpublishing.com

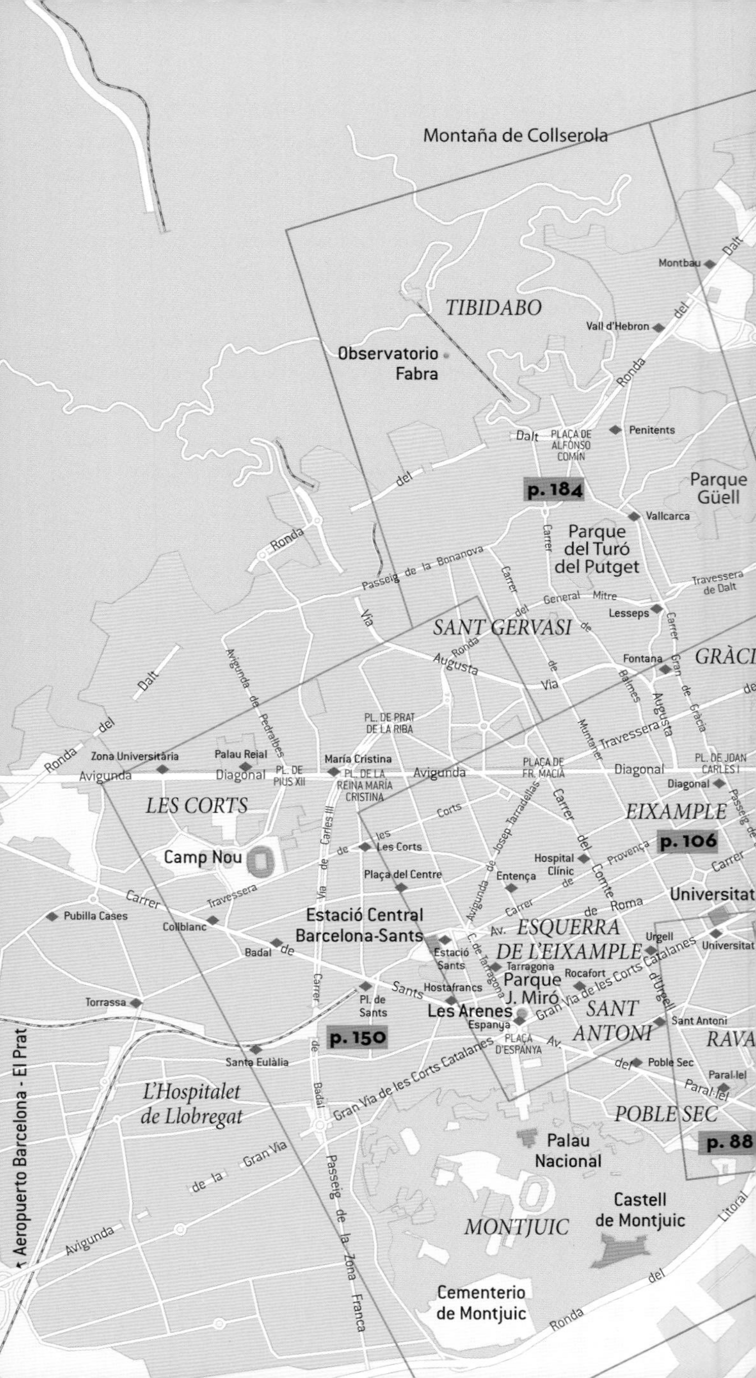
Montaña de Collserola
TIBIDABO
Observatorio Fabra
Montbau
Vall d'Hebron
Penitents
PLAÇA DE ALFONSO COMÍN
p. 184
Parque Güell
Vallcarca
Parque del Turó del Putget
Passeig de la Bonanova
Travessera de Dalt
Lesseps
SANT GERVASI
Fontana
GRÀCI
PL. DE PRAT DE LA RIBA
Zona Universitària
Palau Reial
María Cristina
PL. DE PIUS XII
PL. DE LA REINA MARIA CRISTINA
PLAÇA DE FR. MACIÀ
PL. DE JOAN CARLES I
Diagonal
LES CORTS
EIXAMPLE
Camp Nou
Les Corts
p. 106
Hospital Clínic
Plaça del Centre
Entença
Universitat
Pubilla Cases
Collblanc
Estació Central Barcelona-Sants
Badal
ESQUERRA DE L'EIXAMPLE
Urgell
Estació Sants
Tarragona
Rocafort
Hostafrancs
Parque J. Miró
Torrassa
Pl. de Sants
Les Arenes
Espanya
SANT ANTONI
Sant Antoni
PLAÇA D'ESPANYA
RAVA
p. 150
Santa Eulàlia
Poble Sec
Paral·lel
L'Hospitalet de Llobregat
POBLE SEC
p. 88
Palau Nacional
Castell de Montjuic
MONTJUIC
Cementerio de Montjuic
Aeropuerto Barcelona - El Prat
Ronda del Dalt
Avigunda Diagonal
Gran Via de les Corts Catalanes
Passeig de la Zona Franca
Ronda del Litoral

Can Masdeus
Casa de l'Aigua
Trinita Nova
Santa Coloma
de Gramenet
Trinitat
Vella
Canyelles
Ronda del Dalt
PLAÇA DE
KARL MARX
Via Júlia
Santa Coloma
Valldaura
Passeig de Valldaura
Meridiana
Passeig de Santa Coloma
Baró de Viver
HORTA
Llucmajor
Carrer de Palomar
Torras i Bages
Parque
del Turó
de la Peira
Horta
Passeig de Fabra i Puig
Vilapicina
Virrei Amat
Sant Andreu
Fabra i Puig
SANT ANDREU
EL GUINARDÓ
Maragall
Parque
del Guinardó
Congrès
Verneda
Artigues-
Sant Adrià
p. 202
Guinardó
La Pau
Guipúscoa
Alfons X
Camp de l'Arpa
Navas
Hospital
Sant Pau
Sant Martí
Besòs
Gràcia
Joanic
Provença
Clot
Bac
de Roda
Encants
Sagrada
Família
Sagrada
Família
Besòs Mar
Carrer d'Aragó
Gran Via de les Corts Catalanes
SANT MARTÍ
DRETA DE
L'EIXAMPLE
PLAÇA
DE LES GLÒRIES
CATALANES
Avigunda Diagonal
Selva de Mar
El Maresme
Fòrum
Museu Taurí
Monumental
Glorièś
Parque
de Diagonal
Mar
Poble Nou
Girona
Tetuán
Llacuna
POBLE NOU
Marina
Cementerio
del Poble Nou
Arc
de Triomf
Bogatell
Urquinaona
Arc de Triomf
Playa de la
Nova Mar Bella
LA RIBERA
Parque
del Poble Nou
Parque de la
Ciutadella
Playa de la
Mar Bella
Parlament de Catalunya
Playa del
Bogatell
Jaume I
EL BORN
Liceu
Ciutadella
Villa Olímpica
BARRIO
GOTICO
Estació de França
Barceloneta
p. 10
Drassanes
BARCELONETA
p. 70
Mar Mediterrània
N
0
0,5
1
1,5
2 km

CONTENT

Barri Gòtic

El Born - Barceloneta

El Raval

Eixample

West

CONTENT

North

East

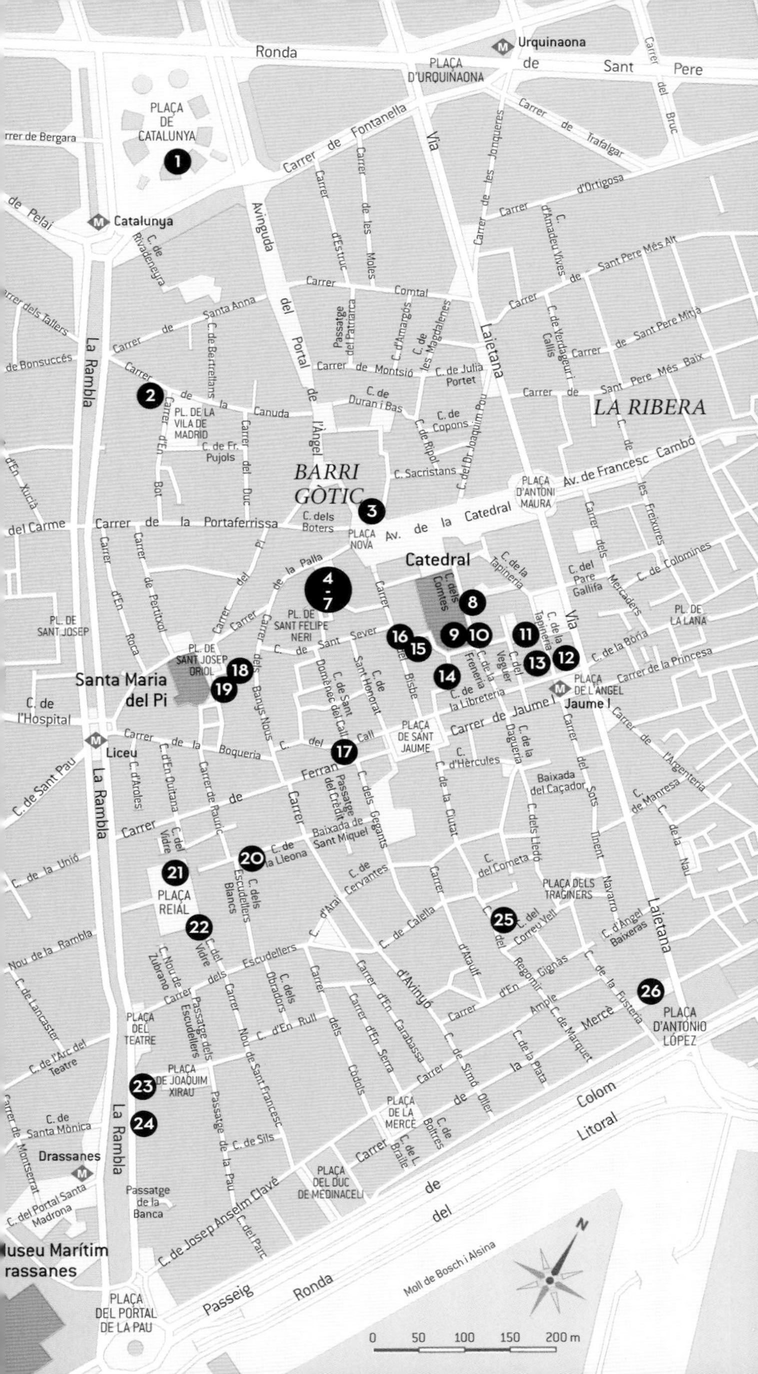

Ronda de Sant Pere
Urquinaona
PLAÇA D'URQUINAONA
PLAÇA DE CATALUNYA
Catalunya
Carrer de Fontanella
Via Laietana
Avinguda del Portal de l'Àngel
BARRI GÒTIC
LA RIBERA
Catedral
PLAÇA NOVA
Av. de la Catedral
PLAÇA D'ANTONI MAURA
Av. de Francesc Cambó
Carrer de la Portaferrissa
Carrer de la Canuda
PL. DE SANT FELIPE NERI
PL. DE SANT JOSEP ORIOL
Santa Maria del Pi
PL. DE SANT JOSEP
La Rambla
Liceu
Carrer de la Boqueria
Carrer de Ferran
PLAÇA DE SANT JAUME
Carrer de Jaume I
PLAÇA DE L'ÀNGEL
Jaume I
Carrer de la Princesa
PLAÇA REIAL
PLAÇA DELS TRAGINERS
Carrer dels Escudellers
Carrer d'Avinyó
Carrer Ample
Carrer de la Mercè
PLAÇA D'ANTONIO LÓPEZ
PLAÇA DE LA MERCÈ
PLAÇA DEL TEATRE
PLAÇA DE JOAQUIM XIRAU
Drassanes
Museu Marítim Drassanes
PLAÇA DEL DUC DE MEDINACELI
PLAÇA DEL PORTAL DE LA PAU
Passeig de Colom
Ronda del Litoral
Moll de Bosch i Alsina
0 50 100 150 200 m
N
1
2
3
4-7
8
9
10
11
12
13
14
15
16
17
18
19
20
21
22
23
24
25
26

Barri Gòtic

STATUE OF THE BLACK MADONNA OF MONTSERRAT

①

A miniature Black Madonna saved from the anarchists

Plaça de Catalunya
Metro Catalunya

As an Eastern proverb says, the protruding nail attracts the hammer. Passing unnoticed and blending in is sometimes the best way to survive.

The Virgin of Montserrat in Plaça de Catalunya is a good example. The story goes that she was saved from the wave of anticlerical fervour and iconoclasm unleashed by the anarchists in Barcelona at the beginning of the Civil War (1936–39), as they failed to even notice her. Otherwise the statue would probably have been melted down or smashed with a sledgehammer. She survived unscathed to comfort many Catholics who murmured a clandestine prayer each time they passed. Today she still stands beside the stone benches lining the square near the Aerobus stop.

The Montserrat sculpture by Eusebi Arnau (1864–1934), of which the Virgin forms part, was installed in 1928 during the work carried out in Plaça de Catalunya for the International Exposition of 1929. The sculpture commemorates Brother Joan Garí, who according to legend was an hermit living in the mountain and was tempted by the devil and committed a horrific murder in the 9th century.

Repentant, he wandered in the mountains of Montserrat, becoming a hermit, eating herbs and drinking rainwater to obtain God's forgiveness, which was granted when the Virgin appeared to him in a mountain cave.

CLUB ATENEU BARCELONÉS

A secret garden and library

Carrer de la Canuda, 6
93 343 6121
ateneubcn.org
Monday to Saturday, 9am–10pm, Sunday 9am–7pm
Members only. Monthly subscription gives access to all Ateneu services: library, meeting rooms, cafeteria
If you only want to visit the romantic gardens, you can ask for a special pass at reception
Metro Catalunya

The Sabassona palace was commissioned by Josep Francesc de Llupià, baron of Sabassona, in 1779. Designed by the architect Pau Mas and listed as a national monument, the neoclassical building was renovated several times in the course of the 20th century. Other than its architectural importance (notably the superb entrance door on Carrer de la Canuda), the palace features the paintings of Françesc Pla ('El Vigatà'), who in the mid-18th century made his name as interior decorator of stately homes and private mansions.

He also designed the romantic garden located 5 metres above street level, a superbly relaxing spot with a wide variety of plants and flowers, in the heart of the Barrio Gótico.

Since 1907 the palace has been home to Ateneu Barcelonés, which defines itself as 'a haven of tolerance, liberty and national culture.'

Apart from the romantic garden and a collection of artworks, the Ateneu has a fantastic library of over 1,000 m^2, open to any students and researchers with an interest in Catalonian history, politics, and society.

Recent renovation work has returned the library to the splendour of its early years (it was founded in 1860).

The repository contains over 300,000 volumes, a great number of incunabula, tens of thousands of historical documents, and special editions dating from the 14th to the 18th centuries. It is one of the most important national collections in Spain.

NEARBY

Watering the horses

The drinking fountains where tourists and local residents come to refresh themselves today were, until the late 1950s, intended for draught animals that pulled the carts carrying merchandise into the city. They were to be found at 77 Vila i Vilá, 40 Carrer del Consell de Cent, and at the junction of Portal de l'Ángel and Carrer del Cucurulla. The oldest (14th century) is the one in Cucurulla. The errand boys responsible for delivering goods in the port area, and in particular the neighbourhoods of El Born and Poblenou, would stop at the water troughs to let the animals refresh themselves, usually leaving them tied up while they themselves drank eau-de-vie or wine in the bars nearby.

BLUE DOG OF 'SANT ROC'

The Barcelona version of the legend of St Roch

Plaça Nova
'Sant Roc' celebrations, on or around 16 August
Metro Jaume I

Not many visitors are aware of it, but today's Avinguda de la Catedral was once a collection of houses, most lost following the Fascist Italian aircraft bombardments of 1938.

At one time, the buildings in front of the façade of the cathedral made up a maze of narrow, windy streets barely penetrated by daylight.

During this period, the focus of relations, trade and celebrations was Plaça Nova, a square that still exists, though it has since been opened up, just opposite the praetorian gateway of the imposing Roman city walls.

That is where the festivities to celebrate 'Sant Roc' (St Roch in Catalan) have been held since the late 16th century.

These are considered Barcelona's oldest celebrations, and are still held every year on or around 16 August, based on the city's very own genuine variation of the St Roch legend.

According to tradition, this devote saint from Montpellier had the gift of healing the sick. His continual contact with the infirm meant he ended up catching leprosy and was shunned by the community, so he took refuge in the nearby woods where a loyal dog brought him a loaf of bread every day until he recovered.

According to the Barcelona version, Sant Roc didn't take refuge in the woods, but lived inside one of the city's two Roman towers, to which the legendary dog took his bread ration every day.

A little chapel devoted to the saint still exists in the tower where he supposedly took refuge, featuring his image.

This figure is a reproduction, given that the original was destroyed in an attack on the clergy during the Civil War. A local picked up the pieces that had been scattered on Avinguda del Portal de l'Àngel and, for a time, they were on display inside a box in the little shrine.

For the reconstruction of the new image, attempts were made to respect the original colours of the old figure as much as possible, which is why the dog is light blue.

According to old folk from the neighbourhood, tradition has it that when the original figure was being made, an extremely indecisive craftsman was chosen for the job, and he kept on asking about each and every detail of the commission he'd been given.

One day he asked what colour he should paint the dog, to which the laconic reply was 'sky blue if it suits you!'

Whether it was because he took offence, or just wanted to stick scrupulously to the specifications, the artisan followed his instructions literally, and even now, far from putting an end to the original dog's colour, the restorers have decided to preserve its traditional appearance. Because a Sant Roc without a blue dog wouldn't be fit to preside over the city's oldest celebrations.

FLAMING HEART SCULPTURE

4

Reminder of the descent of the Holy Spirit ...

Plaça de Sant Felip Neri
Metro Liceu

In Plaça de Sant Felip Neri, above the gate surrounded by walls pockmarked with bullet holes (see p. 24), is a medallion depicting a heart erupting with tongues of fire.

If this sounds familiar to the general public as a traditional Catholic symbol, in this case it refers to an episode in the life of Saint Philip Neri. Meditating in the catacombs of Rome, the saint was suddenly aware of a great light.

Just like Christ's Apostles, he too was receiving the Holy Spirit: a fireball entered his heart, which doubled in size on contact with the flames. This life-changing event is commemorated by the flaming heart symbol (further details opposite).

Saint Philip Neri, whose heart doubled in size as he received the Holy Spirit

Founder of the Congregation of the Oratory, also known as the Congregation of the Filippini after his forename, Saint Philip Neri (1515–1595) was often referred to as the joyful saint because of his cheerful disposition.

Inspired by the early Christian communities, he wanted to anchor an intense spiritual life in a daily routine based on prayer (he was one of the first to gather around him laymen with whom he prayed), reading, meditating on the word of God and praising the Lord, mainly through chant and music. According to him, music was an excellent way of reaching people's hearts and bringing them closer to God, so he was one of the strongest supporters of the revival of sacred music.

In 1544, while the saint was praying in the catacombs of Saint Sebastian over the tombs of the early martyrs, his heart was suddenly seized with immense joy and an intense light shone down on him. Looking up, he saw a ball of fire that alighted on his mouth and entered his chest. On contact with the flames, his heart instantly expanded. The violence of the impact broke two of his ribs. The Holy Spirit had come to the saint, just as it did to the Apostles at Pentecost. In the 17th century, a scientific autopsy on his body confirmed that his heart was twice the size of a normal human heart.

For the saint, nothing would be the same again. The beating of his heart was so strong that it could be heard some distance away and the heat that persistently consumed him meant that he could face the rigours of winter in his shirtsleeves. The symbol of the Congregation today, a heart in flames, is based on this episode of his life.

While looking after the sick, poor and infirm, Saint Philip Neri also took care to spend time with young people in an attempt to stop them feeling bored or depressed. He often gathered a group around him and while always reminding them that life was to be lived joyfully, when the noise became too loud he is supposed to have said: 'Quieten down a bit, my friends, if you can!' His great spiritual gifts even allowed him to bring a young child momentarily back to life.

THE LION OF ST MARK

St Mark, the patron saint of shoemakers, whose guild headquarters were located here

Plaça de Sant Felip Neri, 5
Metro Liceu

The building at No. 5 Plaça de Sant Felipe Neri features a bas-relief depicting a winged lion whose presence is not accidental. This is the symbol of St Mark who, among other things, was the patron saint of shoemakers and the city's guild had its headquarters right here. It may well surprise you to learn that the shoemakers' guild still lives on today and descendants of the old artisans continue to meet up. One little-known oddity is that the Confraria de Sant Marc (Brotherhood of St Mark), linked to the Gremi de Mestres Sabaters (Guild of Master Shoemakers), still includes descendants of the old guild members and is thus one of the brotherhoods with the longest ongoing presence in Europe, dating back to 1202. In fact, the earliest guild chapel was already here in the original Romanesque cathedral cloister, and the saint is still worshipped there to this day, with the feast day of St Mark celebrated to proclaim the new master shoemakers well into the 20th century.

NEARBY

Relief of a shoe

On the side façade of the cathedral looking over Carrer dels Comtes, you can still see the relief of a shoe: this indicates that on the other side of the wall, inside the cathedral, is the old chapel of the shoemakers' guild.

Why is St. Mark the patron saint of shoemakers?

After preaching the Gospel in Italy, St. Mark moved to Egypt, where he became the first bishop of Alexandria. In that city, he founded the Orthodox Christian Church (the Church of the Roman Empire of the East and of the Greek part of the Roman world), ultimately becoming its pope. Captured, he suffered martyrdom in AD 67 because of the number of people he had converted to the faith. His body was then kept in a small chapel in the fishing port of Bucoles (near Alexandria), where he had been killed; from there, it was removed to Venice in a daring 'snatch'. In AD 42, whilst he was in Alexandria, Mark miraculously cured a cobbler by the name of Anianus, who had been seriously injured when repairing the saint's shoes. St. Crispin, a 3rd-century martyr, is another patron saint of shoemakers. He and Crispinian – both cobblers from Soissons – came to Rome towards the end of that century and were beheaded in AD 285 or 286.

See the following pages to learn why the lion has become a symbol of Saint Mark.

Why are there four evangelists?

In the first century AD there were a number of gospels relating the life of Christ, including the gospels of St. Thomas, St. Judas and St. Peter, all of which are now considered to be apocryphal. It was in the second century AD that Irenaeus of Lyons claimed that, just as there were four distinct regions in the world and four main winds, so the Church, which extended throughout the world, should be based on four gospels. The correspondence between the four gospels of Matthew, Mark, Luke and John and the four 'living creatures' (see opposite) probably played a part in these texts becoming the ones that were officially accepted. Others have argued that the so-called apocryphal gospels did not propound ideas concordant with the message that the early Church, largely inspired by the preachings of St. Paul, wished to propagate in order to nurture the growth of Christianity within the Roman world. In fact, some of these texts were considered Gnostic in content, reserving salvation to a few chosen initiates rather than to all mankind. Others presented Jesus not as a God-made-man, but rather as a Jewish prophet-king striving to help the Hebrews free themselves from the yoke of Roman occupation.

The origin of the animal symbols for the four evangelists

In numerous churches around the world, the Evangelists are portrayed alongside an animal:
St. Mark: a lion
St. John: an eagle
St. Luke: an ox
St. Matthew: a man
The explanation for these pairings was given by St. Jerome (348-420) who argued that: St. Matthew was paired with a man because his Gospel begins with the human genealogy of Jesus (Matthew 1:1-17); The lion was associated with St. Mark because the first lines in his Gospel refer to 'the voice which cried in the wilderness', which – St. Jerome claims – cannot be other than the roar of the lion (Mark 1:3); The ox, a sacrificial animal, was associated with St. Luke because his Gospel begins with a reference to the sacrifice offered in the Temple of Jerusalem by Zachariah (Luke 1:5); And the eagle was associated with St. John because this evangelist soared to the very peaks of Christian doctrine, just as the eagle soars to the peaks of mountains.
Historically, the attribution of the four symbols to the evangelists is rooted in the prophet Ezekiel's vision of God in his glory (the four 'living creatures' mentioned in Ezekiel 1:5) and the vision of the throne of God in the Book of Revelation (4:6), which again mentions 'four beasts' around the throne of God: 'And the first beast was like a lion, and the second beast was like a calf, and the third beast had a face as a man, and the fourth beast was like a flying eagle.' Irenaeus of Lyons, in his anti-Gnostic treatise *Adversus haereses* (written around AD 180), was the first to exploit the link of the four evangelists and the four living creatures. As for St. Jerome's explanation, it was first introduced in the Vulgate (his Latin translation of the Bible in the 5th century), which explains why it then became widespread within Western Christendom. In fact, the pairing of evangelists and animals was not accepted by the Eastern Church, which explains why there are very few representations of evangelists with these symbols within Byzantine art. The few exceptions occur where there was an influence of the West – for example, at St. Mark's Basilica in Venice. Another point that St. Jerome makes is that the four living creatures symbolise four fundamental moments in Christ's life: the incarnation of God (man), Jesus tempted in the desert (lion), his sacrifice (ox) and his ascension into Heaven (eagle).

TRACES OF SHRAPNEL FROM THE CIVIL WAR

⑥

Vestiges of the Civil War

Plaça de Sant Felip Neri, 5
Metro Liceu

The façades of several buildings in Plaça de Sant Felip Neri still show the traces of a tragic incident from the Civil War, during which around twenty residents were killed, most of them children.

Historians now agree that these are shrapnel impacts from an aerial bombing by Italian planes that took place on 30 January 1938, although after the war Spanish Fascists tried to claim that they were the result of machine-gun fire from street executions carried out by the Communists.

In this square, surely one of the most peaceful in the city centre, stands the church where the group of children had found refuge, never thinking that a shell would fall through the roof.

At the time, the church was being used as a shelter for children orphaned by the conflict and a photo of their bodies was disseminated throughout Europe, in a vain attempt to persuade the democratic governments to intervene in support of the Republic. The Fascist planes bombing Barcelona were Italian and took off from airbases Mussolini had set up in Mallorca.

Along with Nazi Germany, allies of the uprising against the Republican government introduced a new method of psychological warfare: this consisted of deliberately and continuously bombing non-military targets in residential areas behind enemy lines for intense periods. The goal was to demoralise and terrorise the enemy so that they would surrender. That same method, also implemented by the Luftwaffe in the Basque cities of Gernika (Guernica) and Durango (where there are still traces of shrapnel), was subsequently used widely during the Second World War in the rest of Europe.

THE FACE OF GAUDÍ

Gaudí in the guise of Saint Philip Neri

Church of Sant Felip Neri – Plaça de Sant Felip Neri, 5
93 317 3116
Saturday and the day before festivals: 8.15am–10.15am and 7.15pm–9.15pm
Sunday: 10am–2pm
Metro Catalunya

At the age of 50, the architect Gaudí, who never wanted to be photographed or to appear in newspapers or magazines, agreed to pose for some portraits. One of them is in the Rosary Chapel of the Sagrada Família.

Every day, Gaudí went to the church of Sant Felip Neri to chat with the priest Lluís María de Valls. During the summer of 1902, he decided to pose for his friend, the painter Joan Llimona, for two works that are still kept in the church, one on each side of the presbytery. In the event, the artist chose the features and face of Gaudí to represent Saint Philip Neri in these two paintings.

On the right, Saint Philip Neri with the face of Gaudí is explaining Christian doctrine to some children on Rome's Gianicolo (Janiculum) hill. On the left, the saint, still depicted as Gaudí, is celebrating the Eucharist, the sacrament during which a miracle had occurred and the saint had begun to levitate.

Gaudí apparently said that he supported these works as the Eucharistic sacrifice would save such a sinful city as Barcelona. The Baroque church of Sant Felip Neri was built between 1721 and 1752. Philip Neri, who was born in Florence on 22 July 1515 and died on 26 May 1595, founded the Congregation of the Oratory, which focused on youth, joy and music (for more on the saint, see *Secret Rome* in this series of guides).

JEWISH HEADSTONE IN THE WALLS

⑧

The remains of an old Jewish cemetery

Plaça de Sant Iu
Metro Jaume I

If you're standing in Plaça de Sant Lu and look carefully at the side wall of Palau del Lloctinent (Lloctinent Palace), you'll notice that some of the stones used in its construction (ordered by Emperor Charles V in 1549) are rather odd.

Some people will simply see these as enigmatic symbols, but those familiar with Jewish culture will immediately observe that the characters on the stones are from the Hebrew alphabet. Most passersby, perhaps even the majority of locals, never notice this but the symbolism is important, given the origin of these mysterious stones.

According to one etymological theory, Montjuïc, the hill that overlooks the city on the seaward side, took its name from the term 'mount of the Jews', although another hypothesis is that it originated from the term 'Mont Iovis', referring to Jupiter.

What has been demonstrated archaeologically is that between the Mirador de l'Alcalde and the Tiro Olímpico, there was a Jewish cemetery from at least the 11th century (though it is assumed that it dates from earlier than that) until 1391, following the massacre carried out in the Jewish quarter. Excavations have revealed more than 700 bodies buried in the necropolis and a large quantity of funerary artefacts.

By the time of the construction of Lloctinent Palace, the Jewish quarter had been decimated and, after 1492, with the Catholic Monarchs' order for the expulsion of the Jewish community, in theory there were no more Jews in Barcelona. Jewish streets were given Christian names and (as the cemetery had already fallen into disuse some years earlier) some of the headstones were reused as building materials.

At the bottom of the façade of the building looking out over Plaça del Rei, near the Saló del Tinell (Tinell Hall), there are other stones with Jewish inscriptions. The palace was originally designed to house the viceroy, though it never fulfilled that function.

One of the functions it did carry out was to house the Court of the Spanish Inquisition, hardly the city's finest hour. One of the institution's main occupations was the persecution of those Jews who, although theoretically converted to Christianity, continued to practise their old faith.

NEARBY

On the façade of the Museu Marès, which is on the same square, on the corner of Carrer dels Comtes, we can see the shield of Philip II, crowned by an olive branch, a Christian cross and a sword, which made up the logo of the Inquisition. For a time, the Court of the Inquisition was also housed in this building.

SYMBOLS OF SAINT STEPHEN'S GUILD ⑨

Stoning of the first Christian martyr

Carrer dels Comtes

In the curved wall of the apse in the east wing of Barcelona Cathedral, almost opposite the Marès Museum, are two arresting sculptures. Both of them belong to Saint Stephen's guild, one of the three main medieval guilds, along with those of Saints Eloi and Julian.

They aimed to provide mutual assistance to their members, much like an insurance company today.

These two sculptures allude specifically to the saddlers' guild. The one on the left represents a saddle and a bit, symbols of the craftsmen who made and sold harness.

The second sculpture (see opposite) is a crown of laurels encircling three stone spheres, which commemorates the stoning of Saint Stephen.

Saint Stephen's guild brings together various trades associated with horsemanship and was very influential at the royal court in the 14th and 15th centuries.

The saddlers were highly respected and had their own chapel by the grand altar of the cathedral.

These symbols were carved in this part of the cathedral because it was closest to Carrer de la Frenería where the saddlers used to work.

Saint Stephen, the first martyr

Known as the first Christian martyr, Saint Stephen was one of the seven deacons charged with helping the apostles. He worked tirelessly to convert great numbers of Jews to the Christian faith. Accused of blasphemy against Moses and against God, he was stoned at the outskirts of Jerusalem. There seems to be no particular reason why saddlers are associated with Saint Stephen. In fact, throughout its long history their fraternity had taken responsibility for a wide range of other trades, notably painters, lancers and embroiderers.

For more information about the streets named after guilds in the Barri Gòtic, see the following double pages.

Streets in the Barri Gòtic named after guilds

Daguería (cutlers), Agullers (needle makers), Cotoners (cotton weavers), Espaseria (gunsmiths), Mirallers (mirror dealers), Corders (rope makers), Fusteria (carpenters), Escudellers (shield makers) and Tapinería, where the shoemakers fashioned women's sandals from cork lined with leather and fabric, are just some of the street names in the Barcelona neighbourhood where the medieval guilds settled to ply their trades.

The guilds were family-based organizations or fraternal societies. The three most important of these guilds were the elois, the julians and the esteves, named after their respective patron saints Eloi (Eligius), Julian and Esteve (Stephen). It was not easy to be accepted by a guild, especially as membership was not hereditary.

It was gained by hard work: the apprentices had to respect a whole series of standards and demonstrate their skills in their chosen trade. The tests were difficult as the work had to be exemplary.

For example, if a craftsman decided to use materials of inferior quality, the 'examiners' who went round the workshops would force him to hang the faulty pieces from the shop door, and that would be the end of his reputation.

Although on a practical level the guilds existed to protect the interests of craftsmen, set prices, regulate relations between apprentice and master, and guarantee the quality of products, these powerful bodies maintained close links with the Church, negotiated special privileges with monarchs, and sent representatives to the Council of the Hundred.

In times of danger, the guilds were responsible for organizing the defence of the city. In other words, their influence was not limited to professional matters but had repercussions at every level of medieval Barcelona society.

Guild members did not only have premises in the same street, they also shared tools and the means of production. Moreover, the concentration of a group of craftsmen in the same area was practical for customers. Legend has it that a blind man wanting to know his whereabouts was guided by the smells emanating from the different workshops.

The bonds between the guilds and the Church were evident in the cults devoted to their respective patron saints.

In Spain, Saints Abdon and Sennen were patrons of the gardeners' guild, Saint Peter of the fishermen, Saint John the Baptist of the tanners, while Saint Eulalia was both the official patron saint of

the city and of masons. Doctors and barbers paid tribute to Saints Cosmas and Damian. The blacksmiths were a special case, because the tools of all the others depended on them, as did weapons and chivalrous artefacts. They were protected by Saint Eloi.
These guilds existed for 600 years, until the mid-19th century when capitalism, and especially massive investment in industrial factories, spelled the end of the ancestral trades.

THE BREASTS OF SAINT AGATHA

10

Cruel torment

Capilla de Santa Ágata del Museo Histórico de la Ciudad
Plaça del Rei, s/n
93 315 1111
museuhistoria.bcn.cat
Tuesday to Saturday 10am–7pm, Sunday 10am–8pm
Closed on Monday
Metro Catalunya, Urquinaona, Jaume I, Liceu

Built in 1302 by command of James II of Aragon, the Chapel of Saint Agatha is part of the Roman walls. It is one of the most secluded

religious edifices in the city, upstaged by the neighbouring buildings which include the City History Museum, where an archaeological site has been discovered underneath the buildings: 4,000 m^2 of Roman ruins, among which there is a 3rd-century winery.

In the chapel, the centerpiece is a painting of Saint Agatha holding up a tray on which are placed her own breasts. A little further on, the Condestable Altarpiece, a 15th-century work by Jaume Huguet, evokes the visit of the Magi. To the right of the altar, a small stairway leads to the 16th-century tower of King Martin I (the Humane) of Aragon.

Climbing these stairs, however, demands physical agility in addition to an interest in history.

Saint Agatha

Agatha, a pretty and devout daughter of a Sicilian noble family, was propositioned by the Roman senator Quintianus in the 3rd century, at a time when Christians were being persecuted by the Emperor Trajan. Faced by this Christian virgin's categorical refusal of his advances, he subjected her to the cruellest of tortures. First he sent her into a brothel, but miraculously, she emerged still a virgin. Then she was made to suffer a series of other torments, culminating in the mutilation of her breasts. Agatha was consoled by a vision of Saint Peter, who protected her from pain but not from death. In 250, just one year after her passing, Etna erupted and the islanders called on Saint Agatha to stop the flow of lava. Since that day, Agatha has been the patron saint of Catalonia and Sicily, as well as that of women with breast problems.

A bomb in the history museum

On the night of 7 November 1893, the young anarchist Santiago Salvador went to the Liceu theatre to see a production of Rossini's opera *William Tell*, with two bombs concealed about his person. One of them killed twenty members of the audience in the orchestra pit. The other failed to detonate and is now on display at the City History Museum.

These circular metal bombs bear the mark of Felice Orsini (1819–1858), an Italian revolutionary who attempted to kill Napoleon III with a similar device, when he too was on his way to the opera.

STREETLAMPS IN PLAÇA DEL REI ⑪

Let there be light ...

Plaça del Rei
Metro Jaume I

In the square beside the History Museum are replicas of three medieval streetlamps (there are another two in Plaça de Santa María del Mar).

These lamps used resin as fuel, which ignited readily, took a long time to burn and gave off a pleasant smell.

That was very important at the time and served the same purpose as incense in church – neutralizing the smell that filled any space where a great number of pilgrims were gathered, in the days before deodorants and shampoos.

Around 1725, this type of oil lamp was still being used in Barcelona, but they were only used on special days and worked with wood fuel. A century later, on the evening of 24 June 1826, the feast day of Saint John, gas lamps lit up for the first time the building that houses the former Barcelona stock exchange (Llotja).

From 1842 onwards, the same system began to be used for lighting La Rambla and other streets and squares.

The following year, the Frenchman Charles Lebon planned the construction of the first gas production plant, the Sociedad Catalana para el Alumbrado por Gas (Catalan Gaslight Company), which provided lighting on an industrial scale, especially in the developing new factories.

Electric light was not generally available in Barcelona before 1904, although the beginnings of the electrical industry go back to 1873. In that year, the Barcelona optician and physician Tomás Dalmau and the engineer Narciso Xifrá inaugurated the first electricity generating plant.

The system worked with four gas-powered motors that drove machines each producing 200 voltamperes.

These supplied electricity to various premises in the city. 1888 saw the installation of the first electric lampposts, which were to coexist with the gas lamps until the mid-20th century.

THE ANGEL OF PLAÇA DE L'ÀNGEL ⑫

Saint Eulalia's miracle

Plaça de l'Àngel, 2
Metro Jaume I

At No. 2 Plaça de l'Ángel stands a curious bronze figure, thought to be an angel.

The left arm of this androgynous figure, wingless and bearing a cross on its forehead, is pointing with an outstretched finger to a spot said to be the site of a miracle – the archway in Baixada de la Llibretería, where there used to be a portrait of Saint Eulalia, patron of the city of Barcelona.

Legend has it that in 879 the mortal remains of the saint were being transferred from Santa María del Mar church to the cathedral. Along the way, someone stole one of Eulalia's fingers and, until it was restored, no human force could move the rest of her body.

The sculpture in Plaça de l'Ángel is a replica.

The original, which dates from 1618, is in the City History Museum. The portrait of Saint Eulalia disappeared at the end of the 19th century.

CERERÍA SUBIRÀ

The oldest shop in town

Baixada Llibreteria, 7
93 315 2606
Monday to Saturday 10am–8pm, closed on Sunday

A short distance from Plaça Sant Jaume can be found Cerería Subirá, the oldest shop in Barcelona. Although the shop has been open since 1761, it was renovated in 1847, and the site has been owned by just two families over the 250 years of its existence. Such is its reputation that the churches of Barcelona now buy half its total output.

The other half goes to customers who like decorative candles, which range from Disney characters to more sophisticated creations.

Things have not always gone smoothly for Cerería Subirá but it has coped with various setbacks.

After the Civil War, not many people could see any beauty in a candle – far from seeming romantic or intimate, candlelight was instead a reminder of a time of restrictions and suffering.

REMAINS OF A ROMAN TEMPLE

(14)

Probably not the Temple of Augustus

Paradís, 10
Free entry at the Centre Excursionista de Catalunya, usually closed in winter
Metro Jaume I

In Carrer del Paradís, at the entrance to the Centre Excursionista de Catalunya courtyard, there is a distinctive millstone fixed to the ground and a plaque marking the highest point of the Old City of Barcelona (Mont Tàber, 16.9 metres above sea level).

Here lie the ruins of an ancient temple which was part of the Roman forum, now Plaça de Sant Jaume (today much reduced in size).

Only four columns remain from the original temple, which were located in the upper right corner. However, at some point one of them was taken down and re-erected on Plaça del Rei, only to be subsequently returned to its original location. A section of the architrave has also

survived, though this now forms part of another later construction. The temple was 35 metres long and 17.5 metres wide, with the perimeter columns set on a podium.

These columns, which are the best-preserved Roman ruins in Barcelona, are commonly believed to be the remains of the temple dedicated to the Emperor Augustus Caesar.

In 2007, however, a team carrying out excavations over 35 m^2 in the vicinity of the main access to the nave of Tarragona Cathedral found the foundations and steps of a temple. Experts believe that this is the authentic site of the temple that was dedicated to Augustus in the region.

According to the archaeologists responsible for the dig: 'We cannot categorically state that this temple was dedicated to the Emperor Augustus, but a series of finds leads us to think it highly probable. We have been able to show that this was an octostyle temple (eight columns on the façade) at the centre of an arcaded gallery resembling the architecture of the Forum of Augustus at Rome, dominated by the Temple of Mars Ultor (Mars the Avenger).'

Roman Barcelona

In AD 15, Barcelona was known as Colonia Augusta Faventia Paterna Barcino, or simply Barcino. The existing city was built over the remains of the Roman one, of which several vestiges can still be seen, the most spectacular of which must be the 3rd-century Roman ramparts.

The brick and mortar walls were almost 2 metres thick with a perimeter of 1,250 metres. The 10 hectare area of enclosed ground was coffin-shaped with four entrances (part of one of the gates is in Carrer de Regomir). The ramparts that can be seen today were constructed on the outer face of the earlier ones, to a height of 8 metres. They were equipped with sixty-six towers.

In the Middle Ages, the ancient fortified walls became too confining for the prosperous and expanding city, so King James I of Aragon ordered new walls built, an endeavour that took over a century.

These new walls, which enclosed the principal neighbourhoods of the time, covered an area ten times the size of the Roman city and corresponded to the area now known as the Barri Gòtic.

For more information on the vestiges of Roman Barcelona, see following double-page spread.

Vestiges of Roman Barcelona

1. Roman necropolis – Plaça de la Vila de Madrid.

The tombs have an opening through which relatives could leave flowers and food for their dead. Not far away, a small museum displays relics found in the tombs, such as miniature glass bottles where the tears shed during funerals were collected and coins with which the deceased paid Hades' ferryman to cross the Styx to the underworld.

2. Roman aqueduct – Plaça del Vuit de Març.

In 1988, the demolition of a former parking lot led to the chance discovery of the Roman aqueduct. It had been preserved and used as a dividing wall and corresponds to a small section of four arches some 20 metres long and 4.10 metres high.

3. Porta Decumana – Plaça Nova.

This square was the northern entrance to the Roman city. The two towers and the Roman wall date from the 1st and 4th centuries BC, although the path leading inside was built in 1358. In the left tower is the 1953 recreation of the aqueduct that brought water to the city and which, according to some of the archaeological theories currently undergoing an in-depth reappraisal, featured two courses, one from the Collserola mountain range and the other from the Besòs River.

4. Roman wall – between Plaça de Ramon Berenguer el Gran and Plaça d'Emili Vilanova.

From Plaça Ramon de Berenguer el Gran two types of wall can be seen, Roman (below – 1st century BC, fortified in the 4th century) and medieval (above). This leads to Plaça d'Emili Vilanova, where there is another section of ruins (tombstones, pedestals and sculptures used to strengthen the wall).

5. Temple of Augustus – Carrer del Paradís, 10. See p. 42.

6. Roman gate leading to the sea – Centre Cívic Pati Llimona – Carrer del Regomir, 3.

The southern gate, which remains were discovered in 1984, was the main entrance to the Roman city that led directly to the sea. In 1984, the remains of the gate were discovered.

7. Museu d'Història de la Ciutat – Plaça Reiál.

During the restoration of Barcelona's City History Museum in 1931, extensive Roman ruins were discovered underneath Plaça Reiál. Most of these ruins correspond to agricultural and craft workshops for washing and dyeing, the production of wine and salted fish.

8. Defensive tower – Plaça dels Traginers.

Part of the ruins of the Roman wall with its defensive tower dating from the 4th century.

9. Casal de Gent Gran Pati Llimona – Carrer del Correu Vell, 5.
Within this public facility for senior citizens is an important section of the Roman wall.

10. Demolished wall – Carrer del Call, 7.
Building dating from the 15th century, built on top of the Roman wall. At one place, the ruins of a demolished section of the wall can be seen.

11. Two Roman towers – Carrer d'Avinyó, 19.
Inside a restaurant, in the lower section, are the walls of two Roman towers. Inside the adjacent jewellery store you can see the base of a Roman tower.

12. Centre Sinia – Carrer dels Banys Nous, 16.
Hidden within this centre for disabled people is part of the Roman wall.

13. Domus – Carrer de la Fruita, 2.
Ruins of a Roman house dating from the 4th century and of a taberna (commercial building).

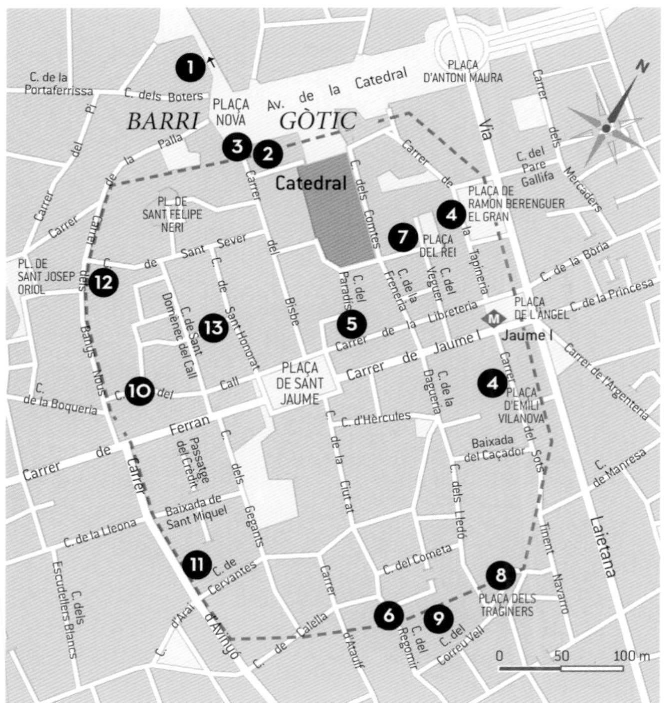

SAINT LUCY'S YARDSTICK

An ancient unit of length?

Carrer de Santa Llúcia 1
Metro Jaume I

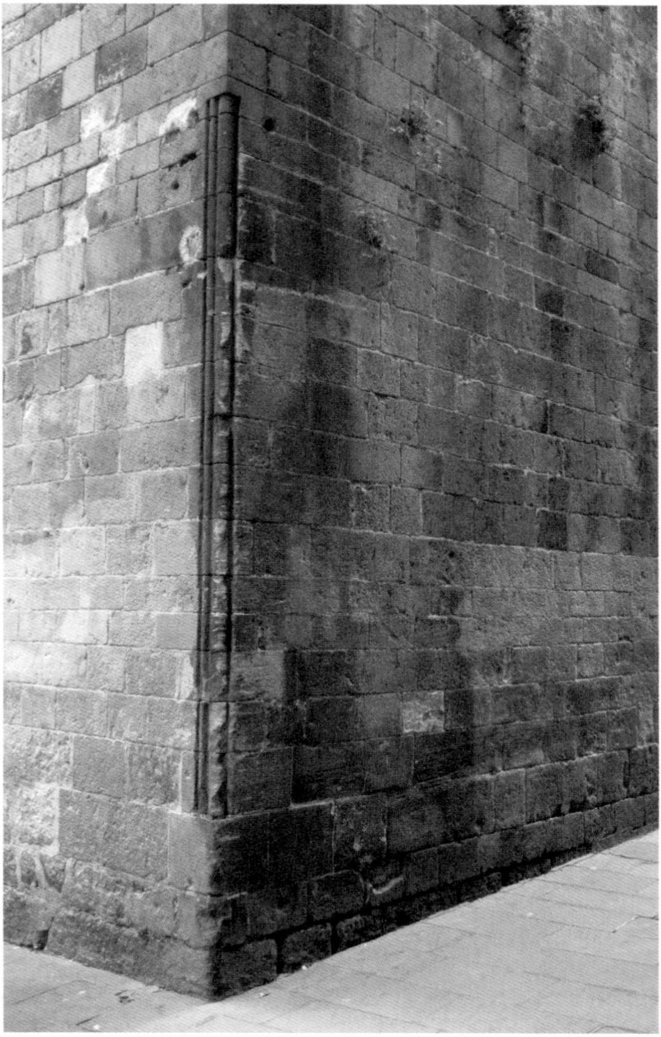

Carved in the stone of an outer corner of the chapel of Santa Lucia is a vertical rod some 1.5 metres long. In the 12th century, it was thought to be the standard for a destre, an ancient unit of length equivalent to eight palms, six feet, or two strides.

At the time, each kingdom used different measures, and in Barcelona the destre was 3.20 metres, about the same as Saint Lucy's yardstick, hence the belief that this was a standard unit of length. In fact, it is not quite eight palms long ...

Some historians think that the carving indicates the water level before the chapel was built.

Another hypothesis is that it was just a whim of the architect.

'LOPOV' INSCRIPTION

A sign marking a neighbourhood well?

Carrer de Santa Llúcia, 1

Near the Cana de Santa Llúcia (see previous double-page spread), on the front façade of the chapel of Santa Llúcia, and also on Carrer dels Comtes where it reaches the Pla de la Seu, if you cast your eyes down to road level you will find an enigmatic inscription reading 'LOPOV'.

As the letter 'V' used to be the equivalent of today's letter 'U', extensive research into possible Latin meanings has generally concluded that the inscription should read 'LO POU', which in Catalan means 'the well'.

This has still to be demonstrated archaeologically but given that Barcelona (and especially the old town centre) had a major water-table supply, which used to feed many of the wells in inner courtyards throughout the area, the inscription might be a form of signage indicating where this water could be accessed.

In fact, during some of the city's sieges, attempts were made to poison the water of the 'Rec Comtal', a network of channels taking it from the river Besòs, to force people to surrender. But the locals continued to drink water from the city's many wells.

Even today, the great quantities of water mean that efficient drainage systems are called for in underground train tunnels and new-builds.

On the façade of the chapel of Santa Llúcia we also find a stone inscription reading: 'A 2 CANAS LOPOV': the two *'canas'* refer to an old Catalan unit of measurement and it is thought that it marked the distance to a supposed well that was found during construction. In spite of every effort, it has not yet been possible to confirm this hypothesis.

PORTRAIT OF FRUCTUÓS CANONGE 17

A celebrated shoeshine boy

Passatge de l'Ensenyança, 1
Metro Jaume I

Fructuós Canonge i Francesch (1824–90), nicknamed the Gran Canonge or Catalan Merlin, is one of the most striking characters in the history of Barcelona.

His family escaped from the poverty of Montbrió del Camp (Tarragona) and moved to Barcelona seven years after his birth. After trying various jobs, he established a shoeshine stall in Plaça Reiál whose sign is still in the porch, near the Colón brewery.

After serving a prison sentence in Cuba for failing to comply with a curfew during the 1856 uprisings, he returned to Barcelona where his sense of humour, eccentricities (he ate shoe-polish to show that it was good quality) and illusionist's tricks (he made cigarettes appear behind the ears of bystanders and broke eggs on the steps to extract gold coins from them) made him famous.

After making his debut in 1858 at the Teatre dels Camps Elisis on Passeig de Gràcia, he became one of the best-known magicians of his time and travelled throughout Spain, France and South America. Doors were opened to him in the top theatres and palaces, and he even performed for Queen Isabella II, Prince Amedeo of Savoy and King Alfonso XII. He received various titles and decorations, including the Cross of the Order of Isabella the Catholic and the Cross of the Order of Charles III, which he always wore proudly on his chest. Between the years 1860 and 1870, he was also the leading light of Barcelona Carnival.

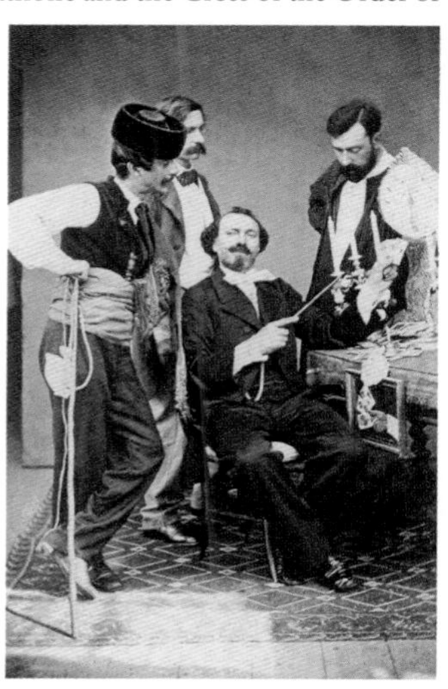

Although he earned plenty of money as a magician, he died in poverty at the age of 66 at his home in Carrer de la Canuda.

In 2003, Barcelona City Council restored the mural dedicated to him in Passatge de l'Ensenyança, where he is shown pulling a rabbit out of his hat.

MURALS AT No. 6 CARRER DE LA PALLA

18

Hidden Modernist murals

Carrer de la Palla, 6
Daily 11am–9pm

As soon as you walk through the doors of the shop at No. 6 Carrer de la Palla, bang in the middle of one of the city's most touristy

shopping areas, you'll be surprised to find a series of murals with a Modernist aesthetic and typography running along the top of the walls. There is also a human figure crowned in laurels in the style of ancient Rome, holding out his hand and looking to the heavens.

Everything would seem to suggest that the murals are the remains of an old paint and lacquer store.

Some Japanese-style cranes flying over the sea are a reminder of Nunoya, the old Japanese textile shop that was here before the current business.

STONE PLAQUE FOR THE MIRACLES OF JOSEP ORIOL ⑲

In spite of his extraordinary obesity ...

Plaça Sant Josep Oriol

In the apse of the church of Santa Maria del Pi a stone plaque reads: 'On 6 April 1806 news arrived of the approval of the miracles of the servant of God Josep Oriol, and to mark the event the outside of this church was illuminated. And on crossing this little raised walkway, the master

builder Josep Mestres fell to the ground without receiving any injury despite his extraordinary obesity, as recorded in the archive of the religious community, and in commemoration of which this plaque was erected.'

It may be hard to understand what really happened without setting the scene, but the first thing to do is note the height of the little walkway running along the top of the apse, and then find out who Oriol and Mestres were. Josep Oriol was an extremely devote native of Barcelona who lived in the city in the 17th century. He was known as a priest with a great propensity for works of charity, and during his lifetime was attributed with thaumaturgy – the working of miracles such as turning slices of radish into coins. He tends to be depicted on a cloud, as seen in the portrayal of him inside the church. For the Roman Catholic Church to canonize a saint, he/she had first to be considered a servant of God, then be beatified and finally, once any miracles carried out during his/her lifetime had been ratified by the Vatican, the aspiring saint could be canonized. Curiously, this very wall features several plaques bearing witness to the process. One, next to the corner of the main façade, is dedicated to the 'Beatus Oriol', then there's the plaque of interest here, naming him a servant of God, and finally the main plaque on the square attesting to his canonization. When the Holy See approved Oriol's miracles, a great celebration was held in the city. Santa Maria del Pi, the parish where the saint undertook many of his great works, was a rival of Santa Maria del Mar, and both churches put up a large number of decorative lanterns and there were reports of processions and fireworks. It was in that context that the cathedral master-builder Josep Mestres i Garmatxes, due to his large size, clumsiness and quite possibly the few tipples he may have had to celebrate the canonization, fell from the walkway. Without receiving any injury, let's not forget, despite his extraordinary obesity …

THE INITIALS CNT-FAI

Vestiges of the anarchists from the Spanish Civil War

Back wall of the Church of Sant Jaume
Carrer de la Lleona, 9 bis
Metro Liceu

On the back wall of the Church of Sant Jaume, you can still read the letters CNT-FAI flanking one of the windows. These are the last vestiges of the building's seizure by anarchists during the Spanish Civil War.

By 19 July 1936, Barcelona was abuzz with rumours about possible military action in favour of the coup aimed at bringing down the Republican government. A section of the army, with the support of conservative forces, had launched the coup in other cities the previous day.

On 19 July, some soldiers left their barracks and advanced into the old town. There they were surrounded and neutralised by the forces of law and order, along with trade union workers and left-wing party members: the government had armed them, fearing that their officers would be unable to combat the uprising on their own.

In some cities, such as Pamplona, Burgos and Valladolid, the coup was successful whereas in others, including Barcelona, Madrid, Valencia and Bilbao, the Republic managed to beat back the insurgents. Within one day, towns and cities found themselves either under government

control or that of the organisers of the coup, with the country divided into zones depending on which side had a decisive advantage. And so began a bloody civil war that would last until April 1939.

In light of the euphoria generated by the local victory, the streets of Barcelona were taken over by workers' forces, largely led by the anarchist trade union the CNT (Confederación Nacional del Trabajo: National Confederation of Labour) and its allied subgroup the FAI (Federación Anarquista Ibérica: Iberian Anarchist Federation), which favoured direct action.

Either because they supported the coup or for fear of reprisals from the revolutionary forces that had taken over the city, many wealthy locals fled to areas under the control of those who sided with the uprising, abandoning their properties, many of which were seized by the workers' forces.

Vehicles carrying the militia around the city quickly started to appear on the streets with the letters CNT-FAI, UGT, PSU, POUM, etc. daubed on them with paint. Some luxury hotels were converted into community kitchens, and churches and mansions were used as warehouses, libraries or boarding houses for refugees pouring into the city from areas where the coup had been successful.

After Franco's victory in the Civil War, the dictatorship took repressive measures against those who had opposed the uprising. The painted signs on the walls of seized buildings were removed, though just a few, like this one, are still visible today.

GAUDÍ'S STREETLAMPS

21

Of the six lamps designed by Gaudí, only four remain

Plaça Reial, s/n
Metro Drassanes

Pla de Palau, s/n
Metro Barceloneta

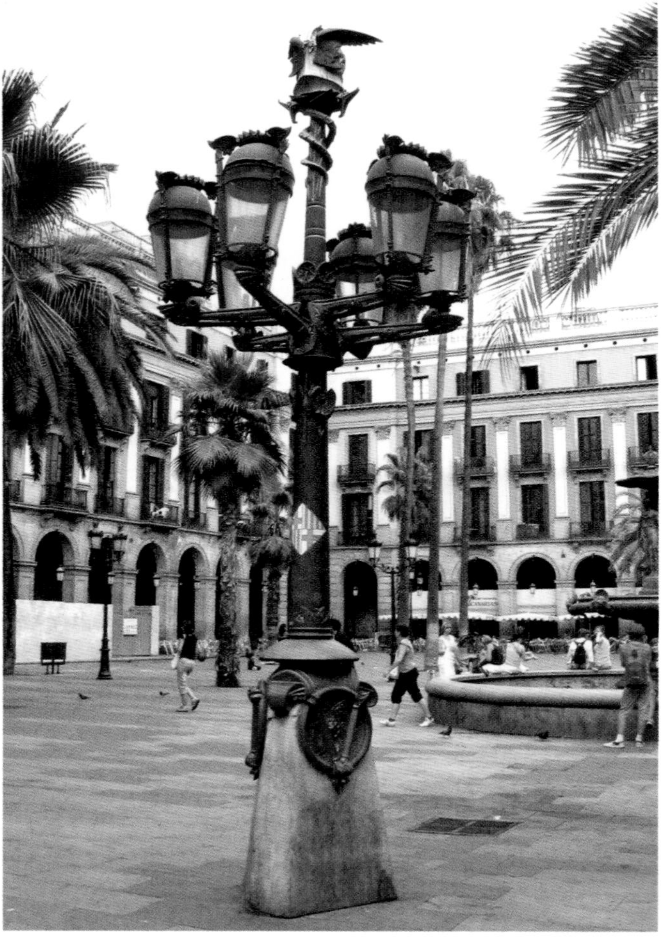

© Canaan

The *fanals* (lamps) in Barcelona's Plaça Reiál are quite amazing and worth a closer look. They were designed by the Modernist architect Antoni Gaudí i Cornet (1852–1926) as one of his first commissions in 1879. This was a month before he graduated as an architect and started work as a designer with Josep Fontserè, a Freemason like himself, which probably explains why he was given this commission.

Gaudí designed two different types of lamp, one with three and the other with six branches. Two of these lamps, with a stone base and bronze and wrought-iron posts, grace Plaça Reiál. However, given their high price (3,500 pesetas at the time), Barcelona City Council wanted the others to be cheaper. Gaudí simplified the design so that each lamp would cost no more than 1,500 pesetas, but after that he no longer wanted to work for the council, despite its insistence on trying to appoint him as official architect. Minimalism had no place in his extravagant style.

The decoration of the upper section of the Plaça Reiál streetlamps is particularly striking, featuring the Roman god Mercury with winged helmet and two snakes coiled around the centre post. These lamps were installed in September 1879.

The location of the lamps between the Masonic lodges of General Madoz and Ildefons Cerdà is an interesting detail, hinting at the fact that Gaudí was probably a Freemason.

In 1890 the three-branched lamps, also in pairs, were installed in front of the municipal buildings in Pla de Palau. Of Gaudí's six lamps, the two originally in Paseo Juan de Borbón in the Barceloneta neighbourhood are missing. Nobody knows where they are now. The official explanation is that they are 'lost'.

© Canaan

HARE KRISHNA TEMPLE

(22)

After lunch, you can visit the temple ...

Plaça Reial 12, entresuelo 2
93 302 5194
Daily
Metro Liceu

The Hare Krishna temple opens its dining room everyday to anyone who accepts its conditions: there is no set menu, you eat whatever is on offer that day, but it is strictly vegetarian, consisting of salad, soup, main dish, dessert, and water. No other drinks are available.

The main entrance is very discreet – there is no notice board, just a doorplate. Inside, the ambience is festive, with incense floating in the air and joyful background music. The dining room has a small terrace and large windows that bathe the place in light.

After lunch, you can visit the temple: a very spacious hall that you must enter barefoot, dominated by a life-size statue of the founder of the world Hare Krishna movement, A.C. Bhaktivedanta Swami Prabhupada. Both the meal and tour are informal, as are the Sunday open days, aimed at attracting new members.

Who are Hare Krishna?

The group known as the International Society for Krishna Consciousness (ISKCON) preaches a faith based on traditional Vaishnava Hinduism, practises bhakti yoga, and worships the god Krishna (literally 'principal deity'). Inspired by the teaching of the Bengali saint Caitanya Mahaprabhu (1486–1533), the name of the movement comes from the words of the maja mantra (main prayer) chanted by its adherents. In 1966, Abhay Charanaravinda Bhaktivedanta Swami Prabhupada took his teachings to New York, where he set up a base from which to promote and sell his books in airports and on the street, rapidly increasing the number of followers. Hare Krishna devotees routinely live apart from their families, believe in reincarnation, and refuse to touch alcohol, tea, cigarettes, meat, or eggs. They do not gamble and sex is for reproductive purposes only.

TRACES OF PROSTITUTES 

Streetwalkers' legacy

La Rambla, 22 y 24

The two indentations you can see through the glass door of the entrance to the restaurant at Nos 22 and 24 on La Rambla are not there by chance: They were made by the prostitutes who, over a number of years, paced backwards and forwards on this spot, waiting for clients. Over time, the pressure of their heels wore down the marble and left these indentations for posterity. In 1956, prostitution was banned by the authorities and brothels were closed. Prostitutes were thus forced to seek out their clients on the street and especially, as was the case at Nos. 22 and 24, at the doors of small hotels.

For many years, the bottom end of La Rambla near the port was a favourite place for buying and selling sex, but the practice was stamped out in the runup to the 1992 Olympic Games. The municipality and the Friends of the Ramblas association invested millions of pesetas to renovate the area.

Love hotels

'Love hotels' hire out rooms by the hour. They are intended for couples and are the opposite of bad taste. Many of them are boutique hotels, designer-decorated to satisfy the sexual fantasies of their guests. In other words, they have round beds, mirrored ceilings, adult TV channels and jacuzzis.

La França is one of the largest and most renowned love hotels, boasting more than 70 luxury rooms and private parking where guests looking for complete anonymity can have their number plates covered with a discreet cloth. In the Raval district, in the heart of central Barcelona, we find La Paloma Hotel, which is fresher and more modern and affordable. Regàs Hotel offers a similar service, but in the Gràcia area.

These three hotels – and in general all hotels offering couples rooms by the hour – have a set of very specific conditions. To start with, guests can stay in their rooms as long as they like but once they've left a room they cannot go back to it. You do not need to book in advance, as the idea is that guests can check in at any time. Gay couples are welcome but threesomes are strictly forbidden.

La França: La França Xica, 40 – 93 423 1417 – lafransa.com
Hotel Regàs: Regàs 10–12 – 93 238 0092 – hregas.com
Hotel La Paloma: La Paloma 24–26 – 93 412 4381 – hlapaloma.com

A SECTION OF THE MEDIEVAL WALL HIDDEN IN A CAR PARK

24

Remains of the city's second walled enclosure

Interparking La Rambla
La Rambla 20
93 301 1142
interparking.es
Open 24 hours
Metro Drassanes

The name of Barcelona's legendary 'Rambla' originates from the Arabic words *'ramla'* or *'riera'*, meaning rainwater channel or riverbed.

In the Middle Ages, the layout of this iconic avenue was the 'Riera d'en Malla' which, particularly in times of heavy rainfall, collected the water coming down from the Pla, or plateau, of Barcelona.

In the 13th century – by which point the city had long since swallowed up the Roman walls, with more inhabitants now living outside them than inside – 'Riera' became the geographic boundary delimiting the city's second walled enclave.

This enclosure remained intact until it became obsolete once the city walls of Raval had been built. For many years it stood as the symbol of a Barcelona split in two: Ribera, which housed the political, financial and administrative centres, and Raval, an area given over to farming, hospitals and charitable institutions.

The Rambla wall had several gateways, one of which was Trentaclaus, located where Plaça del Teatre stands today. During the construction of the underground car park there, builders uncovered the sole surviving visible remains of the old Rambla wall, now part of the sides of the car entrance and exit ramps.

A wall that saved the people of Barcelona

In 1714, after the troops of Philip IV had laid siege to the city for more than a year as part of the Spanish War of Succession, and once the assailants had managed to enter the city where hand-to-hand skirmishes were now taking place, the Duke of Berwick called for the city's unconditional surrender. General Pau de Thoar went to talk terms and threatened to continue fighting in the other part of the city, protected by the Raval walls.

Faced with the obstinacy of the populace, and the fact that Berwick wanted to put a victorious end to an attack on the city that had gone on much longer than expected, he agreed to negotiate terms of surrender. This meant disobeying the king's orders (which were to 'put them all to the sword'), so the terms were never signed and sealed by the monarch. But when the military leader finally conquered the city, he took it upon himself to stop all pillaging and abusive practices that had taken place in the other towns and cities conquered by his troops.

CAPELLA DE SANT CRISTÒFOR DEL REGOMIR ㉕

Blessed be your car ...

Regomir s/n
93 301 7433
Friday 7pm–8pm
Car blessing: 10 July
Metro Jaume I

Each year on 10 July, all of the taxis in Barcelona queue up to have their vehicle blessed at this tiny chapel built in 1503. The chapel, dedicated to Saint Christopher, patron of travellers in general and taxi drivers in particular, was the first in the country to bless vehicles.

The drivers recall that during the 1970s, when the number of motorists in the city increased dramatically, as many as 2,000 vehicles could be seen waiting their turn for the blessing.

The tradition goes back to 1906, when Cristofol Sarrias, a pharmacist in Carrer de Regomir, and his friend Carles Bonet introduced the French custom of blessing vehicles on Saint Christopher's feast day. Only four cars were present at the first ceremony, one of them belonging to the artist Ramón Casas and another to the writer and painter Santiago Rusiñol.

Holding at most twenty people, Saint Christopher's chapel is so small (only two rows of chairs) that the font is outside the building in order not to hinder the flow of worshippers.

Nearby, at the junction of Carrer de Montcada and Carrer dels Carders, is the equally small 12th-century Marcus chapel, named after the philanthropist Bernat Marcus who built a hospital specializing in the treatment of travellers and pilgrims.

St Christopher, patron saint of global travellers

Before he became a saint, St Christopher was called Reprobus. He was tall, blond, stocky and blessed with a friendly, outgoing nature. He was a great adventurer, with a huge desire for glory. He therefore decided to offer his sword in the service of a great king. He defended the Romans and fought the Persians until he heard of a certain Jesus Christ, more powerful than any king. He wanted to serve him and was guided by the advice of a hermit. For many years, he helped the weak and the sick to cross a wide and fast-flowing river until one day a very heavy child arrived. That day the waters were particularly rough and with each step the child weighed more. Having crossed the river, a feat which almost cost Reprobus his life, the child confessed that he was in fact Jesus and that from that time on his guide would be called Christophorus, which means bearer of Christ. Christophorus, or Christopher, devoted the rest of his life to defending Christianity from the pagans. He was finally beheaded. It is said that one of his arms is preserved in Santiago de Compostela and part of his jaw in Astorga.

CORREOS, THE PHANTOM METRO STATION

(26)

The lights from a phantom station can still be seen from the street

Plaça Sant Antoni López, s/n
Metro Jaume I

When Barcelona began to expand in the late 19th century, Via Laietana, known as Via A, was built to lead from the city to the sea and it incorporated tunnels planned for the future metro.

The first phase of the Barcelona metro brought it to Jaume I station, the intention being to have the terminus at Francia station.

Following technical and financial problems, it was finally decided to extend the metro to Correos, which was nearest the sea at the time. Correos station opened on 20 February 1932.

Then in 1966 the metro was extended to Barceloneta and, given the proximity of Jaume I station to the sea, Correos lost its usefulness and was closed for good on 20 March 1972.

The former corridor is still used as a ventilation shaft, as can be seen through the gate to the right of the entrance nearest to Via Laietana.

This abandoned station is also lit up at certain times, so it is easy to see from above, via the ventilation shaft that opens onto the street.

You can also see the phantom station inside the metro, from the carriage windows, between Jaume I and Barceloneta stations.

Other phantom stations in Barcelona

Line 1: Bordeta
Line 3: Fernando y Travessera
Line 4: Banco (this one was never opened or accessible from street level but the stairs are still there)
Line 5: Gaudí
In the Ferrocarrils de la Generalitat, Avinguda de la Llum

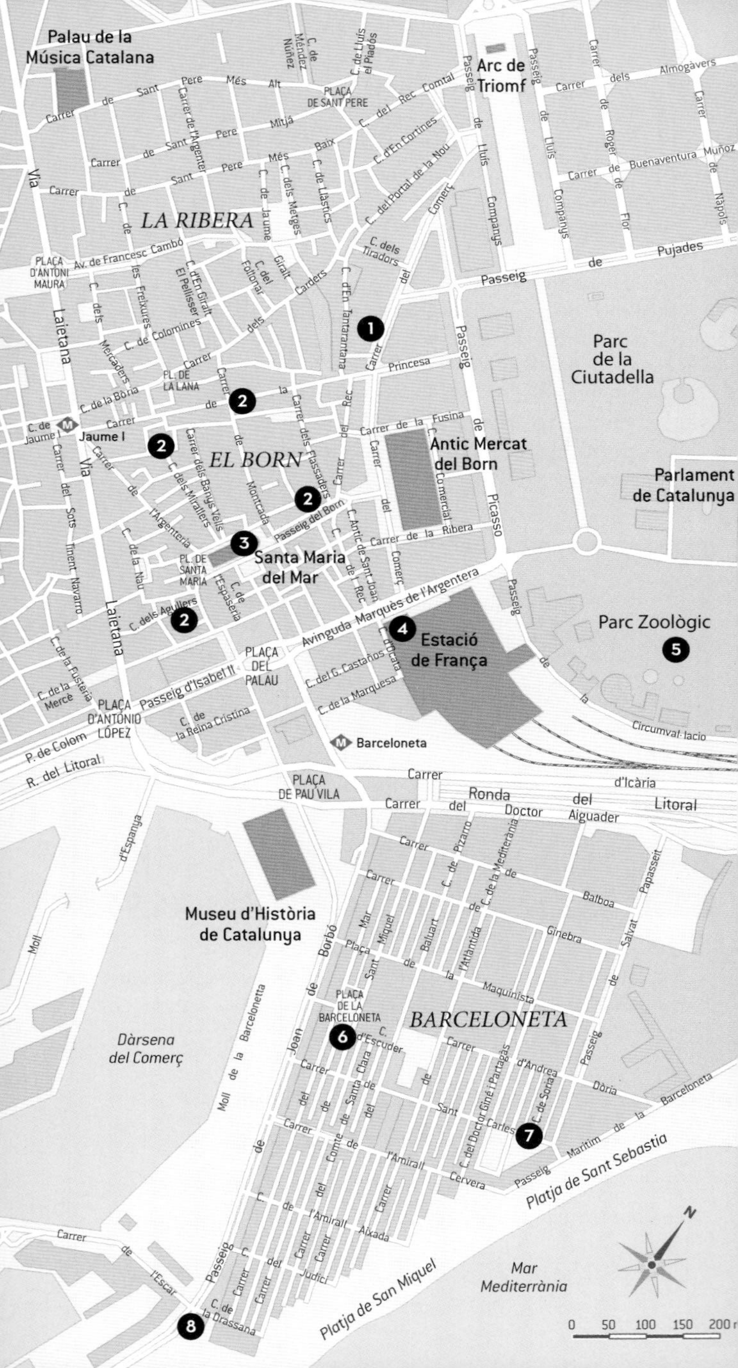

Palau de la Música Catalana
Arc de Triomf
LA RIBERA
EL BORN
Parc de la Ciutadella
Antic Mercat del Born
Parlament de Catalunya
Santa Maria del Mar
Estació de França
Parc Zoològic
Jaume I
Barceloneta
Museu d'Història de Catalunya
BARCELONETA
Dàrsena del Comerç
Mar Mediterrània
Platja de Sant Sebastia
Platja de San Miquel
PLAÇA D'ANTONI MAURA
PLAÇA DE SANT PERE
PL. DE LA LANA
PL. DE SANTA MARIA
PLAÇA DEL PALAU
PLAÇA D'ANTONIO LÓPEZ
PLAÇA DE PAU VILA
PLAÇA DE LA BARCELONETA
Via Laietana
Passeig de Lluís Companys
Passeig de Pujades
Passeig de Picasso
Passeig de la Circumval·lacio
Avinguda Marquès de l'Argentera
Passeig d'Isabel II
Ronda del Litoral
Passeig de Joan de Borbó
Passeig Marítim de la Barceloneta
Moll de la Barceloneta
Moll d'Espanya
1
2
3
4
5
6
7
8
0 50 100 150 200 m
N

El Born - Barceloneta

MASONIC SYMBOLS AT SANT AGUSTÍ MONASTERY

①

Napoleonic lodge symbols

Comerç, 36
93 310 3732

Freemasonry came to Spain when Napoleon's troops invaded in 1808, and various lodges were subsequently set up. The king imposed on Spain by France, Napoleon's brother Joseph Bonaparte, was the Grand Master of French Freemasonry.

Napoleon's supporters and the Masons of Spanish lodges proclaimed the First Republic in 1873, with the motto 'Liberty, Equality, Fraternity' taken from Freemasonry and the French Republic.

They placed the Masonic symbols, including the square and compasses, on the three gates of Carrer del Comerç. In the early 1960s the symbols disappeared from the tympanum of what is now the entrance to the Chocolate Museum. On the central door, you can still see the initials F and M for freemasonry.

Tradition holds that the first Augustinian Christian community was established in Barcelona thanks to Saint Paulinus of Nola's visit to this city. He was ordained as a priest in 393, apparently under pressure from his followers. It is said that he founded a community, traces of which predate the Saracen invasion. This is thought to have been originally in Sant Pau del Camp and later to have found a permanent home in Barcelona.

In 1309 the Augustinians settled in Carrer del Comerç, on land donated by citizen Jaume Basset, a site now known as Sant Agustí Vell; they laid the foundation stone of the church in 1349. Construction of the monastic buildings was not complete until the 18th century.

The bombardment in 1714 during the War of the Spanish Succession damaged the monastery and in 1716 Philip V of Spain ordered its demolition to make way for his citadel. The Augustinians then settled near Carrer de l'Hospital.

The ruins of the building on Carrer del Comerç were restored by Pere Bertran (1738–48) and subsequently converted into bread ovens. The building was used as an army barracks and recruiting office from 1750 until the late 20th century. You can still see architectural elements from the former monastery, notably the restored west wing of the cloister (1473–78). Part of the building is now a civic centre, alongside the Chocolate Museum and municipal offices.

During the 19th century, a series of incidents threatened the community and its resources. In 1808 the building was taken over by Napoleon's troops and for a time soldiers and monks cohabited, but the monks left in 1813. The following year, the troops also abandoned the monastery, but the monks soon returned and started restoration work. However, they had to endure accusations of collaboration with the occupying forces. In 1835 the monastery was set on fire, as were the city's other religious buildings.

For more information about the symbolism of the square and compasses, see the following double pages.

Masonic symbolism of the square and compasses

The square, used in construction to measure angles, can also teach us to 'act with rectitude, in accordance with Masonic law, and to harmonise our conduct following moral principles and virtue'. The square, which is the symbol of the Apprentice Mason, serves to transform a rough stone into a polished one, often representing matter, and pointing to the 'rectitude of action'. The compasses, meanwhile, with their adjustable setting, symbolise the mind and determine how we 'measure our search'.

Anyone who pays close attention will realise that, though the two tools tend to appear together, they are not always arranged in the same way, and that is significant. The position of the square over the compasses refers to the first Masonic level, that of the Entered Apprentice. At that point, matter (the square) is still predominant over the mind or spirit (the compasses).

When the tools are interlinked, they refer to the second Masonic level, that of the Fellow Craft, a level where the individual is evolving and matter and spirit are in equilibrium, a necessary condition for attaining spiritual enlightenment.

When the compasses are on top of the square (as in the Place Paul Langevin, in Paris' 5th *arrondissement*; see *Secret Paris*, also published by Jonglez), that means that the spirit (spirituality) has vanquished matter (the profane), a progression of the individual's initiation into the Masonic hierarchy marked by the third level, that of the Master Mason.

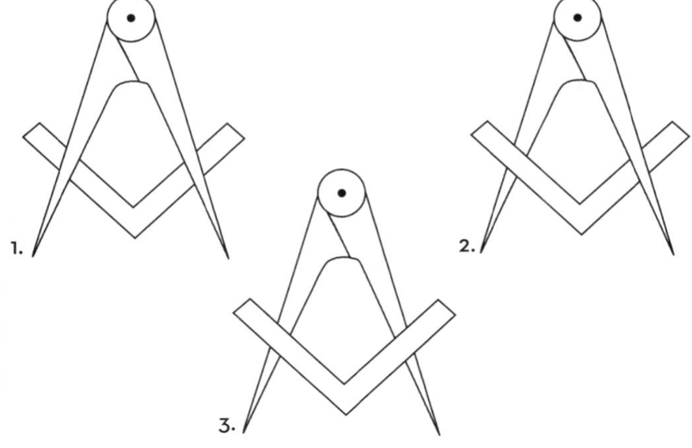

SCULPTED FACES IN EL BORN ②

Signs of 15th-century brothels

Junction of Carrer de les Panses and Carrer de les Mosques
Carrer Del Arc de Sant Vicenç Carrer Agullers and Carrer Mirallers
Metro Barceloneta

In El Born district various faces of women or satyrs can be seen carved in the walls.

These *carassas* (a Catalan word for gargoyles, although these are more like mascarons or grotesque masks) indicated to travellers or soldiers passing through town the whereabouts of the nearest brothel. The best-known *carassa* is a satyr below the third balcony of a building in Carrer de las Panses, at the corner of Carrer de las Moscas, a narrow alley that cuts through to the only nearby brothel. The three others are in the streets of l'Arc de Sant Vicenç, Agullers and Mirallers.

Being a port city, Barcelona was visited by hundreds of sailors and foreigners who set off in search of these pleasure houses as soon as

they came ashore. The stone faces were the perfect marker, good for foreigners sniffing around as well as the illiterate.

In 1400, a number of brothels were already tolerated and protected by the government.

The prostitutes worked every day of the year except for the Feast of Corpus Christi and Holy Week. At such times they shut themselves up in their workplaces and covered their bodies so as not to expose the faithful to temptation. They could also retire to a convent behind Santa Creu hospital, which was incidentally where they lived out their days when they grew too old to work – they had to be over 20 before starting.

In fact, the walls of the city's earliest brothels were painted red, the colour of passion. Over time, one custom that became extremely widespread was to include the face of a satyr or medusa as a symbol indicating that it was a den of iniquity. There was no other way of doing so, given that many people could not read at that time.

These brothel markings became particularly popular from the 17th century onwards.

FC BARCELONA SHIELD

③

Barça in church

Basilica of Santa María del Mar
Plaça de Santa María del Mar, s/n
Metro Jaume I

On the left of the high altar in the basilica of Santa María del Mar, in one of the windows that in theory date from the medieval Gothic period, a 50 cm by 40 cm Barcelona Football Club shield is displayed.

The shield is the work of artist Pere Canóvas Aparicio, who explains: 'This dates from the time when windows damaged or destroyed by the Civil War were restored or replaced. Several windows were ordered from the company where I work as an artist. Some of them are new creations featuring my drawings, others have been restored. For this we were sponsored by a number of organizations. In the late 1960s, it was the turn of this window. Through the textile industry, we contacted Agustí Montal Jr, president of FC Barcelona at the time, who authorized the club to donate 100,000 pesetas, equivalent to about 12,000 euros today. To thank the club, its shield was incorporated in the window. The other windows also feature the insignia of their patrons.'

Why does Barça celebrate its victories around Font Canaletes?

The Canaletes fountain (133 Rambla de Canaletes) gained its reputation several centuries ago, at a time when chlorine was not added to drinking water so it just tasted of pure water. The fountain's water ran from a spring through the channels (*canaletes*) of an aqueduct and was of excellent quality. It is said that when the locals wanted visitors to settle in Barcelona they would inevitably take them to taste this water, which made them fall in love with the city and bound them to it forever.

The upper stretch of La Rambla has always been one of the best places in Barcelona to quench your thirst. As large crowds tended to gather there, the end of the 19th century saw small shops opening up where drinks and sodas were sold. In 1908, Esteve Sala, an enterprising businessman and keen supporter of FC Barcelona, set up a new drinks stall next to the fountain that soon became a fixture for other supporters.

In the 1930s, the fans renewed their interest in this corner of the city – when the team was playing away, journalists from the sporting paper *La Rambla* (founded in 1930 by Josep Sunyol, another Barça supporter) wrote the result of the match on a blackboard hung in the window of the editorial offices overlooking Rambla de Canaletes, just above the Nuria bar.

Crowds of fans were anxiously waiting in the street below, and if luck was on their side they took the opportunity to celebrate the victory in style.

The newspaper folded after the Civil War and the drinks stall disappeared in the early fifties, but the habit of celebrating sporting victories at Canaletes has endured.

FRIENDS OF THE RAILWAY ASSOCIATION

④

Miniature trains

Estació de França (south entrance) – Carrer d'Ocata
93 310 5297 – aafcb.org
Tuesday, Thursday and Friday 6pm–9pm, Saturday 5pm–9.30pm
Metro Barceloneta

Founded in 1944, Barcelona's Friends of the Railway Association (Asociación de Amigos del Ferrocarril de Barcelona) is a dream come true for rail lovers. Located in the south wing of the França station, it occupies three vast rooms.

One holds the library and has specialized magazines, films, and over 4,000 volumes available to members. Collector's items are found in every available space: signals, telegraph machines, old posters, and hundreds of model trains, replicating both famous and little-known engines.

The second hall is open to members who want to run their model trains and feel like real train drivers. The tracks twist and intersect in such a way that the enthusiastic operators must be on their guard and employ some basic skills to avoid an accident in miniature. Finally, there is a conference hall where lectures and courses are held, and rail films and documentaries projected.

The most striking aspect of this room is the seating, both for conference participants and the general public, which comes from authentic rolling stock. The association, in collaboration with the Renfe/ADIF rail company and the Catalan Government Railways, organizes special outings to discover vintage and modern trains. The AAFCB also has its own collection of vintage trains, such as the Garrat 106 steam locomotive dating from 1926, the Berga 31 steam train from 1902 fitted with wooden carriages, and the Patxanga 304 electric train from 1926. During May, June, July, and August, trips on these trains are organized to nearby villages, where a stop is usually made for lunch, the idea being to recreate the ambience of an earlier age. The association can be visited without pre-booking if you are just passing through. If you wish to join and participate in their conferences, excursions, or become a model train driver, the inscription fee is €30 and the annual fee €98.

There is a similar organization in Paris, with premises located beneath the Gare de l'Est (see *Secret Paris*, in the same collection as this guide).

REPLICA OF MONSERRAT IN BARCELONA ZOO

⑤

A popular 19th-century European custom

Zoo de Barcelona
Parc de la Ciutadella
936 394 752
zoobarcelona.cat
Daily from 10am to sunset

In the section housing Alpine animals in Barcelona Zoo there is a rocky formation reminiscent of a popular Catalan mountain. Emulating other European parks, the Parc de la Ciutadella (created in the 19th century above what was a fortress with a particularly unsavoury history) was opened with a collection of animals that would eventually become Barcelona Zoo.

At the time, European parks would often include a mountain feature from their local area. Whereas in other parks you might find the Alps or some other popular mountain range, in the case of Barcelona, as the capital of Catalonia, there could only be one contender. So where

the zoo stands today, an impressive 20-metre-high reconstruction of Monserrat was built, intended to serve as a vantage point.

Despite being hollow, the structure is remarkably well preserved and is listed as a Cultural Site of National Interest. It was inaugurated on 24 September 1892. The artificial rock formation was extremely popular in its day, becoming a favourite spot for celebrities to have their photos taken. Pablo Picasso particularly admired it and the Picasso Museum has several of his works depicting the Ciutadella's replica of Monserrat.

For many years the mountain was inaccessible as some of the zoo's facilities were built around it and it adjoined several animal enclosures, meaning it stopped being a first-rate tourist attraction and was largely forgotten.

In addition to the reproduction of Monserrat, various Barcelona gardens, such as Parc de l'Oreneta, or Torreblanca in the city's outskirts, have rocky formations that are reminiscent of Monserrat or, more specifically, the Holy Cave of Monserrat, with a space for putting an image of La Moreneta. This custom also became popular in old rural constructions, or *masias*, throughout Catalonia.

There are also reproductions of the Moreneta of Monserrat in more modern buildings, for example on the façade of No. 26 Carrer de Tamarit.

INSCRIPTION: 'CARRER D'EN MIQUEL PEDROLA'

⑥

The remains of a Civil War street name

Corner of Carrer Sant Miquel and Carrer Escuder
Metro Barceloneta

On the corner of the Barceloneta district's Carrer Sant Miquel and Escuder, an old inscription painted directly onto the wall reads 'Carrer d'en Miquel Pedrola'. This is one of the city's last vestiges of a Civil War street name, most of which disappeared during the Franco years.

Miquel Pedrola i Alegre was a local lad who led one of the first militia 'centurias' (divisions of 100 soldiers) that departed for Aragón to halt the advance of Franco's troops.

There he met his death in the attack on a mill near Tierz, which had been taken by the Falangists, when a bullet hit a hand grenade held by one of his fellow militiamen.

When his remains were brought back to Barcelona, his comrades decided to name a street from his neighbourhood after him as a tribute. So Carrer Sant Miquel was officially renamed Carrer d'en Miquel Pedrola, with his name painted on the walls and plaques put up in his honour.

During the Franco years the street went back to its original name, the plaques were taken down and the letters with his name were painted over.

With the return of democracy, the paint on the wall of No. 45 Carrer Sant Miquel started to peel off, revealing the old inscription in honour of militiaman Pedrola.

It was in 2009 that investigations began into the story behind the change in street name, and it was also then that renovations to the building meant that the wall was about to be repainted.

Within a year, the swift actions of historians, with the support of residents from the neighbourhood, led to the Town Council allowing a private company to restore the old painted inscription, revealing its original form.

When the story appeared in the media, a branch of Pedrola's family contacted the researchers, informing them that the militiaman had had a daughter exiled in France, with whom they had lost contact. It turned out when the militiaman died aged just 20, his partner María Valero was pregnant. Their daughter, born in Barcelona, went into exile in France with her mother and grandparents. Following extensive investigations through diplomatic channels, a French historian discovered her whereabouts. Amada Pedrola, Miquel's daughter, got in touch with Pino Suárez and Dani Cortijo, the historians who had studied her father's story, and together they travelled to Aragón to retrace his final footsteps. They are still in contact to this day.

THE HAND OF BARCELONETA ⑦

A mysterious sculpture

Carrer Sant Carles, 35 at the juction with Carrer Soria, 18

To this day there is no known explanation of the origin of the mysterious hand sculpted in stone at the corner of Sant Carles and Soria streets. Located 3 metres above ground level, the palm of the hand faces downwards and incorporates two triangles that indicate opposite directions. Perhaps it was a bricklayer's joke or a stonemason's whim, no one knows for sure. But it has survived over the years and succesive restorations of the building.

The construction of Barceloneta started in 1753 and is the work of the military engineer Juan Martín Cermeño.

At first the houses had only one floor, until 1838, when a second floor could be added. In 1868 a third floor was authorized, and in 1872 a fourth. The house with the hand of Barceloneta dates from 1875.

A ROOM WHERE *IT ALWAYS RAINS* SCULPTURE

8

Five characters in a cage

Plaça del Mar, at the end of Passeig de Joan de Borbó
Metro Barceloneta

As part of the Cultural Olympiad of 1992, Barcelona City Council commissioned eight urban sculptures from eight well-known artists to grace various areas of Barceloneta and Ribera. Some of these works, such as *Homenaje a la Barceloneta* (Tribute to Barceloneta), installed by the German artist Rebecca Horn on the sands of Barceloneta, have become authentic symbols of the city.

Others, however, have passed completely unnoticed by tourists as well as locals – such as the sculpture *Una habitación donde siempre llueve* (*A Room Where it Always Rains*), despite being the work of the Madrid artist Juan Muñoz (1953–2001), one of the best-known sculptors of the second half of the 20th century.

The work features five anonymous figures, immobilized from the waist down in metal spheres, oblivious to one another. They are shut inside a wooden structure reminiscent of the umbraculum of Ciutadella Park, set among the trees a few metres from the beach. These bronze beings seem to evoke the anguish of modern man, the isolation of those who suffer from loneliness while being so close to others, the melancholy of those who feel exposed to the elements in a world full of comforts.

In their apparent silence, the statues of Juan Muñoz challenge, ask questions and send a worrying message ... Is this why so many people pass by on the other side?

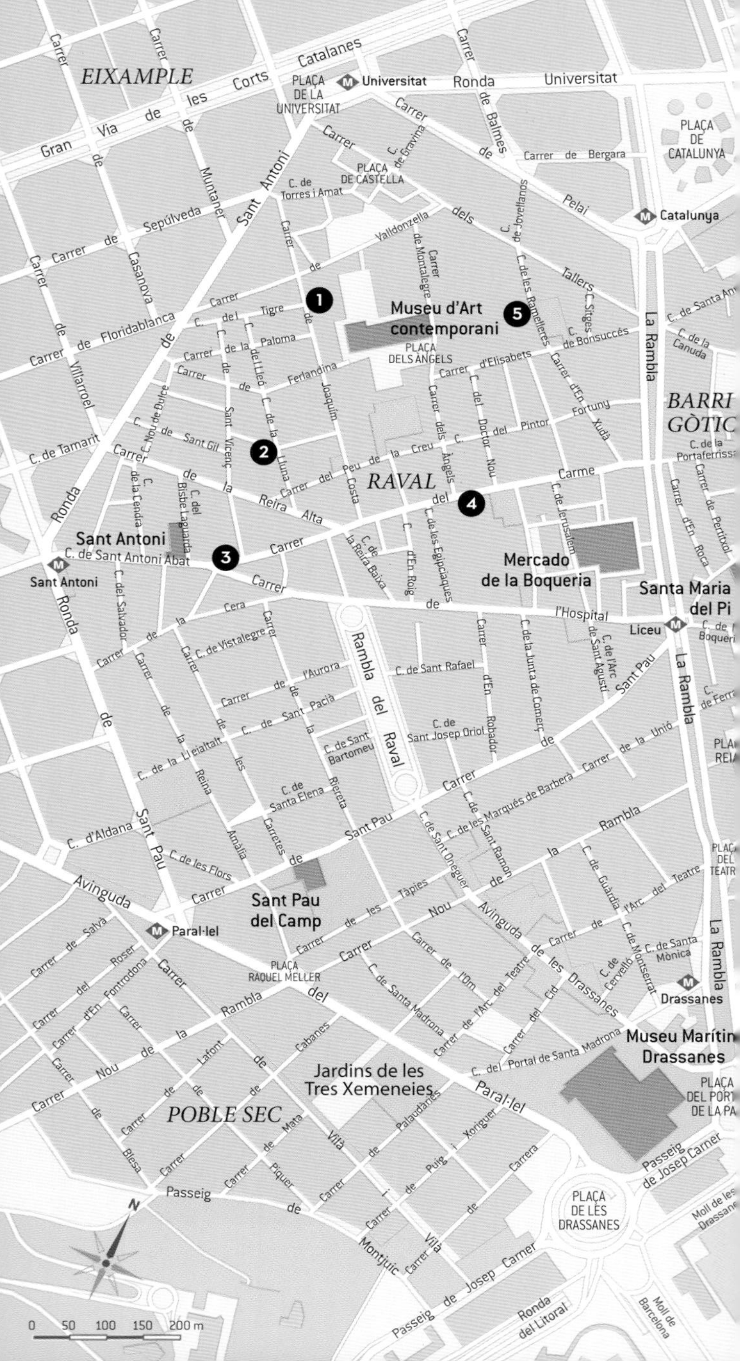

EIXAMPLE
RAVAL
BARRI GÒTIC
POBLE SEC
Gran Via de les Corts Catalanes
PLAÇA DE LA UNIVERSITAT
Universitat
Ronda Universitat
PLAÇA DE CATALUNYA
Catalunya
PLAÇA DE CASTELLA
Carrer de Pelai
Carrer dels Tallers
Carrer de Bergara
Carrer de Balmes
Ronda de Sant Antoni
Carrer de Sepúlveda
Carrer de Floridablanca
Carrer de Muntaner
Carrer de Casanova
Carrer de Villarroel
C. de Torres i Amat
Carrer de Valldonzella
C. del Tigre
Carrer de la Paloma
Carrer de Ferlandina
Carrer de Joaquím Costa
Carrer de Montalegre
C. de Jovellanos
C. de les Ramelleres
C. Sitges
C. de Bonsuccés
C. de Santa Anna
C. de la Canuda
Museu d'Art contemporani
PLAÇA DELS ÀNGELS
Carrer d'Elisabets
Carrer dels Àngels
C. del Doctor Nou
Carrer d'En Xuclà
C. del Pintor Fortuny
C. de Sant Gil
C. de Sant Vicenç
C. de la Lluna
C. Nou de Dulce
C. de Tamarit
Carrer del Peu de la Creu
Carrer de la Reira Alta
Carrer del Carme
C. de l'Hospital
C. de la Reira Baixa
C. d'En Roig
C. de les Egipcíaques
C. de Jerusalem
Mercado de la Boqueria
Santa Maria del Pi
C. de la Portaferrissa
Carrer de Petritxol
Carrer d'En Roca
Sant Antoni
C. de Sant Antoni Abat
C. del Bisbe Laguarda
C. de la Cendra
C. del Salvador
Carrer de la Cera
C. de Vistalegre
Carrer de l'Aurora
C. de Sant Pacià
Rambla del Raval
C. de Sant Rafael
Carrer d'En Robador
C. de la Junta de Comerç
C. de l'Arc de Sant Agustí
Liceu
La Rambla
C. de Sant Josep Oriol
C. de Sant Bartomeu
C. de la Riereta
C. de la Lleialtat
Carrer de la Reina Amàlia
Carrer de les Carretes
C. de Santa Elena
Carrer de Sant Pau
Carrer de la Unió
C. de les Marqués de Barberà
C. de Sant Oleguer
C. de Sant Ramon
Rambla
C. d'Aldana
Ronda de Sant Pau
C. de les Flors
Sant Pau del Camp
Avinguda del Paral·lel
Paral·lel
Carrer de les Tàpies
Carrer Nou de la Rambla
C. de Guàrdia
Carrer de l'Arc del Teatre
PLAÇA DEL TEATRE
C. de Santa Mònica
C. de Cervelló
C. de Montserrat
Drassanes
Avinguda de les Drassanes
PLAÇA RAQUEL MELLER
Carrer de l'Om
C. de Santa Madrona
Carrer de l'Arc del Teatre
Carrer del Cid
C. del Portal de Santa Madrona
Museu Marítim Drassanes
Carrer de Salvà
Carrer del Roser
Carrer d'En Fontrodona
Carrer de Blesa
Carrer de Lafont
Carrer de Cabanes
Jardins de les Tres Xemeneies
Carrer de Vilà i Vilà
Carrer de Mata
Carrer de Piquer
Carrer de Palaudàries
Carrer de Puig i Xoriguer
Carrer de la Carrera
Passeig de Montjuïc
PLAÇA DE LES DRASSANES
Passeig de Josep Carner
Moll de les Drassanes
Moll de Barcelona
Ronda del Litoral
N
0 50 100 150 200 m
1
2
3
4
5

El Raval

EN LA PRENSA DE AQUEL DÍA... ①

An original gift

Joaquim Costa, 44
93 302 5996 – periodicosregalo.com – info@periodicosregalo.com
Monday to Thursday 10am–6pm, Friday 10am–2pm, closed on Saturday and Sunday
15 July–15 August: Monday to Friday 10am–2pm, closed on Saturday and Sunday
Metro Universitat

If you were born on 30 June 1974, did you know that a UFO flew over Barcelona that very day and made the front page of the Spanish newspaper *La Vanguardia*? And that on 22 October 1969, the first landing strip in Antarctica was inaugurated? Reading the papers of the last 100 years is addictive. En la prensa de aquel día ... ('In the press that day ...') has them all in stock, or almost all, as some dates are so popular that they run out.

This archival service was a natural consequence of the owner wondering how to make use of a vast quantity of old newspapers. She later acquired other titles and the small collection became an important historical archive.

Most of the people who come into the shop want to know what happened on the day of their birth (or that of a loved one), or perhaps the day of their marriage.

So the staff rummage through the stacks of old magazines (vacuumwrapped to protect them from humidity) until they find the relevant date.

You can choose between just the front page, the complete publication, or even an advertisement.

The shop also sells another original gift: personalized crosswords. All you have to do is supply a few details about the person you want to surprise: date of birth, tastes, habits, good and bad qualities, or whatever else you can think of to form the basis of an entertaining puzzle.

BULLET MARKS ON THE WALL OF A BUILDING

2

Civil War gunshots on Carrer de la Lluna

Corner of Carrer de la Lluna and Carrer de Cardona
Metro Sant Antoni

On the corner of Carrer de la Lluna and Carrer de la Cardona, lost in the maze of streets making up the Raval district, you can still see traces of gunfire from the Spanish Civil War (1936–39).

Historians haven't been able to establish the date of the altercation or the identity of the shooters, but they do support the version of some locals who claim it was a stalk and kill operation by a sniper from the third-floor window of the building overlooking Carrer de la Lluna.

From that vantage point the whole length of the street can be watched from the corner of Peu de la Creu up to Ferlandina, and Carrer del Lleó up to Valldonzella, as well as Carrer Cardona and Carrer de Guifré, from the corner of Sant Vicenç up to Joaquín Costa. A perfect lookout spot.

The bullet holes indicate that the shots came from the street and were aimed up at the window, while the number of holes would suggest that the shooters were militiamen with limited firearms experience.

The shoot-out may have occurred during one of the bloodiest and most decisive episodes in the conflict, the so-called May Days of 1937, which led to the final split between the workers and anti-Fascist forces. On the one hand the Catalonian government's forces of public order, with the support of the Stalinist militias of the Unified Socialist Party of Catalonia (PSUC, Partit Socialista Unificat de Catalunya), the Workers' General Union (UGT, Unión General de Trabajadores) and the pro-independence party Estat Català, and on the other the anarchist militias of the National Confederation of Labour (CNT, Confederación Nacional del Trabajo) and the Iberian Anarchist Federation (FAI, Federación Anarquista Ibérica) with the support of the Workers' Party of Marxist Unification (POUM, Partit Obrer d'Unificació Marxista). These fratricidal clashes resulted in 500 dead and over a thousand injured, so it's extremely difficult to ascertain on which side either the Carrer de la Lluna sniper or the street-level assailants were on.

THE GENERAL'S BOARDING HOUSE

3

Where an innkeeper was summoned to military headquarters

Plaça del Pedró, 8
Metro Sant Antoni

In the middle of the Raval district's Plaça del Pedró – one side of which marks where Carrer de l'Hospital meets Carrer del Carme, while the other leads on to Carrer de Sant Antoni Abat, which had a gate bearing the same name – the house at No. 8 is clearly older and lower than the rest.

It currently functions as a bar/restaurant but in the past it has served as a dairy and apothecary's shop. Even further back in time, according to local folklore picked up by neighbourhood resident historian Joan Amades, the place was known as the Hostal del Carmen.

Due to its location at the entrance to the city, next to the Portal de Sant Antoni, it was considered one of the best inns in the area and served the constant influx of travellers coming to the city for business.

It dates from the 18th century, at which time most of the current Raval district consisted of farmland and welfare institutions belonging to the church. At the beginning of the 19th century, after the Napoleonic invasion, King Ferdinand VII betrayed the liberals who had put him back on the throne after the French invaders had been defeated. He set about repressing them severely, joining the Holy Alliance, the great defenders of absolutism. At a time when the monarchy was pushing for a return to absolutism, Charles d'Espagnac (known locally as Carlos de España) was appointed Captain General of Catalonia, with the job of applying a firm hand to an unruly land whose capital, Barcelona, had a tendency towards revolt.

Carlos de España was known for his cruel and authoritarian excesses, even towards his own troops, who often asked for him to be removed. His mere presence would make anyone sweat given the ease with which he demanded executions for the slightest offence.

During his rule, he issued an order for inns to stop serving at 8pm and not a minute later. As Amades tells the tale, one day just before 8 in the evening, a man dressed as a vagabond entered the inn. Some locals took the innkeeper to one side, telling him that the beggar looked very like the Captain General of Catalonia, Carlos de España.

Once inside the inn, the man asked to be served supper, at which the innkeeper tried to make him see sense, explaining that he would hardly have time to start eating before he had to call last orders and empty the bar. Faced by the guest's insistence, and as he had given him fair warning, the innkeeper did serve him a plate of food, but he had barely taken a bite before he had to politely ask him (followed by a few pushes) to vacate the premises. The next day, the innkeeper was summoned to military headquarters, where he encountered the much-feared General Carlos de España, who gave him an ounce of gold in return for his strict compliance with his orders, adding that he could count on him as a good friend for all future needs.

According to Amades, this was why the locals of his grandparents' generation gave the inn the nickname 'Hostal del General'.

ANATOMY LECTURE HALL

4

Barcelona's secret masterpiece of neoclassical architecture

Real Academia de Medicina
Carrer del Carme, 47
93 317 1686
Wednesday, 10am–1pm
Metro Liceu

Designed by the surgeon Pere Virgili and built in 1760 by Ventura Rodríguez, the P. Gimbernat anatomy lecture hall of Barcelona's Royal Academy of Medicine and Surgery is a a little-known masterpiece of neoclassical architecture.

This dark and gloomy place has an atmosphere that can be overwhelming, inviting silence and inspiring respect. The circular hall, while not very large, has a very high ceiling. In the centre stands a marble table equipped with a hole to drain away the blood of the bodies being dissected. Its proximity to the Santa Creu hospital of course made it easier to perform demonstrations on human corpses.

Notable among the operations carried out at the time (1770) was the spectacular separation of Siamese twin boys.

The benches where the students sat surrounded the dissection table. In the front rows were a dozen wooden armchairs reserved for the authorities.

A chandelier hangs from the ceiling and between the high windows are busts of a number of immortal figures from Barcelona's medical world, such as Ramón y Cajal, Servet, and Mata.

The building was initially home to the College of Surgery, then until 1904 served as the Faculty of Medicine. It subsequently become a training school and, since 1920, has belonged to the Royal Academy of Medicine. In 1951 it was listed as a historic and artistic monument of national interest.

Once a year, Catalan writers meet in the lecture hall to 'dissect' the Catalan language, discuss the changing vocabulary, the future of the language, and additions to the dictionary.

Visiting is very restricted, with public access on Wednesday mornings only. It is no use trying to get in at other times.

There is a similar hall in London – see *Secret London: An Unusual Guide*, in this collection of guidebooks.

Anatomical theatres through history

An anatomical theatre (*Theatrum Anatomicum* in Latin) is a room dedicated to the teaching of human anatomy to medical students. The first ever amphitheatre was built in 1594 at the university of Padova (Italy), but Greek physician Herophilus of Chalcedon was already performing public dissections on human corpses at the Alexandria School of Medicine in Egypt in the year 300BC. These dissections were initially forbidden then later authorised again during the Renaissance in western countries.

During the 15th century, dissections were performed in small improvised rooms, such as in the former hospital of the Royal Monastery of Santa María of Guadalupe (Spain), home to a prestigious medical school that trained famous surgeons and was granted a papal bull to perform anathomías or dissections.

The discoveries of the great anatomist Vesalius (1514-1564) marked the beginning of a new era. During the 16th century, anatomy became a very popular discipline not only among students, but also with the wider public. The first temporary anatomical theatres in Italy were based on a structure similar to that of amphitheatres of the Roman Empire. When dissections were abolished, the theatres were systematically destroyed. French anatomist Charles Estienne – known as Carolus Stephanus in Latin and Charles Stephens in English – later introduced a new architectural style in Paris, which remained very popular until the 19th century.

As the study of anatomy evolved, permanent anatomical theatres emerged. During the 16th and 17th centuries, two different design models came to the fore: those of the university of Padova and those of the university of Bologna. While both models incorporated wooden constructions within the largest building of their university, their architectural characteristics diverged.

In 1594 the first permanent anatomical theatre of the University of Padova was created by Girolamo Fabrici of Acquapendente; it took the form of a funnel (a truncated inverted cone) and could welcome up to 200 visitors. The theatre was in use for 278 years before being transformed into a museum. It became the reference model for a number of other amphitheatres: Leiden (Netherlands, 1597); Uppsala (Sweden, 1620); Copenhagen (Denmark, 1640); Groningen (Netherlands, 1654); Kiel (Germany, 1666); Amsterdam (Netherlands, 1691); Altdorf (Germany, 1650); Berlin (Germany, 1720); and Halle (Germany, 1727).

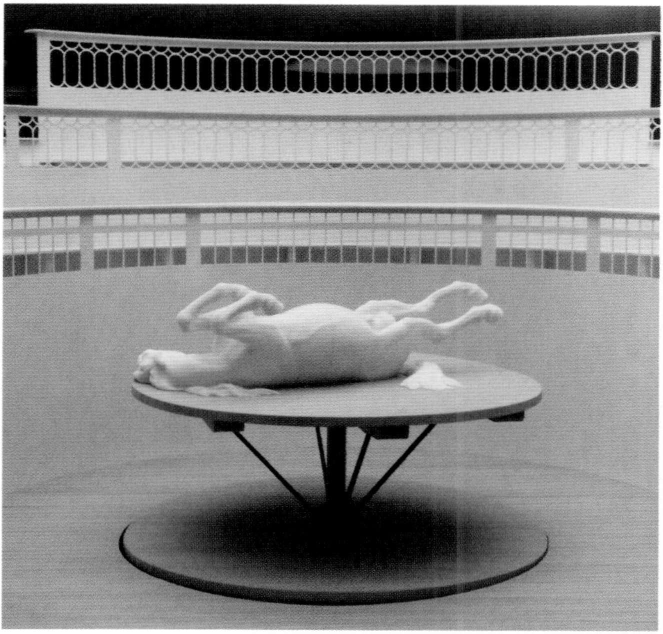

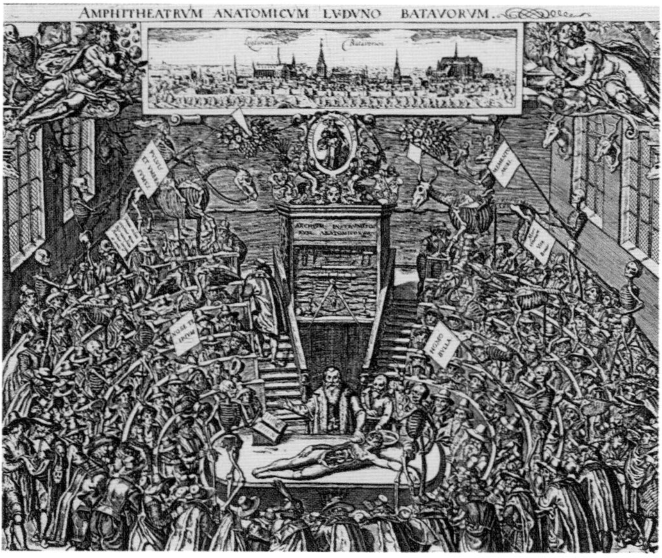
AMPHITHEATRVM ANATOMICVM LVDVNO BATAVORVM.

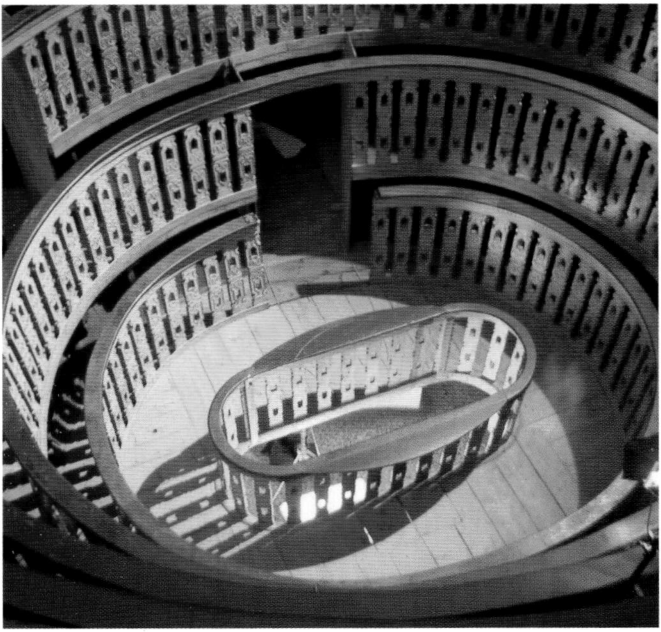

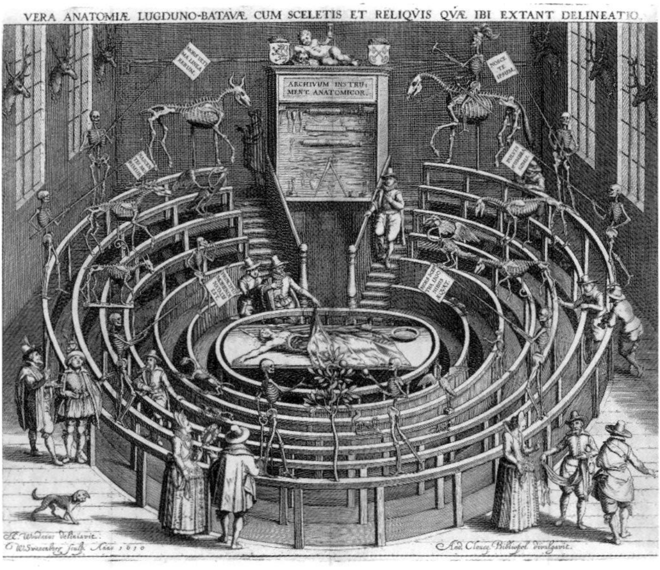

VERA ANATOMIÆ LUGDUNO-BATAVÆ CUM SCELETIS ET RELIQVIS QVÆ IBI EXTANT DELINEATIO.
ARCHIVUM INSTRU: MENT ANATOMICOR.
NOSCE TE IPSUM.

The other main architectural style for permanent amphitheatres followed that of the amphitheatre of Bologna, built in 1637 by the architect Antonio Paolucci. Rectangular in shape, like many medieval meeting places, it was decorated with magnificent wooden panels and sculptures depicting famous physicians of history. One anatomical theatre influenced by the Bologna model is the theatre of Ferrare (1731).

During the 18th century, considerable modifications were made to the structure of anatomical buildings. The first autonomous anatomical theatre was built in Saint-Côme (France) by the Royal Academy of Surgery of Paris in 1694. The academy later became the École de Chirurgie (School of Surgery) and relocated to another building built by architect Jacques Gondoin. The design of the Grand Amphithéâtre (1768-1775) was influenced by the Pantheon in Rome, particularly apparent in its cul-de-four vault and demi-rose window. It could accommodate more than 1,400 visitors. In such a monumental environment, the corpse on the table and the professor performing the demonstration appeared almost in miniature. The school building was intended to evoke a sanctuary dedicated to Asclepius, the Greco-Roman god of medicine.

New methods for the preservation of human corpses required additional space to ensure the storage, preparation, maceration, investigation and exhibition of the corpses. All these requirements meant that the relevance of the traditional *Theatrum Anatomicum* was limited.

Nevertheless, a number of notable new theatres were built during this era: Barcelona (1762); Frankfurt (1776); Mainz (1798); Montpellier (1804); London (1822); Erlangen (1826); Munich (1826); Dorpat (1827); Göttingen (1828); Tübingen (1832); Zurich (1842); Greifswald (1854); Berlin (1863); Fribourg (1867); Bonn (1872); Leipzig (1875); Prague (1876); Rostock (1876); Strasburg (1877); Breslau (1897); Marburg (1902); Basel (1921); Helsinki (1928); and Sofia (1929).

The evolution of audiovisual equipment gradually led to a revolution; anatomical auditoriums eventually became mere screening rooms. In 1872 the German physiologist Czermak (1828-1873) built what he called the 'Spectatorium' in Leipzig. This institute, which comprised modern and comfortable audiovisual rooms, marked the definitive end of the traditional *Theatrum Anatomicum*.

EL TORN DELS ORFES

5

Drop off your children ...

Carrer Ramelleres, 17
Metro Catalunya

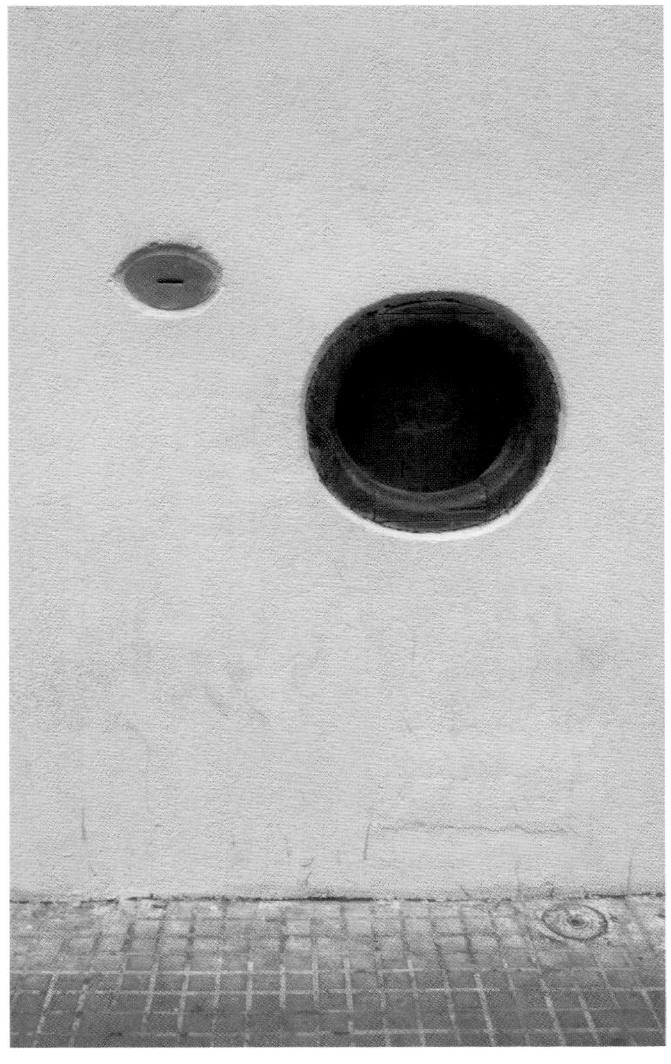

At No. 17 Carrer de les Ramelleres, you will see what looks like a hole in the wall. Known as *El torn dels orfes* ('The orphans' hole'), this was where the much-despised single mothers of former times abandoned their babies to the care of the nuns.

The Casa de la Misericòrdia, founded in 1583 at Plaça de Vicenç Martorell, 300 years later became the *Casa Provincial de Maternidad y Expósitos* (Provincial Home for Expectant Mothers and Waifs). The hole, a sort of pivoting window into which the babies were placed, was in service from the mid-19th century to 1931. The building has since been renovated and converted into the administrative headquarters of the Ciutat Vella district.

The hole, however, has been preserved as being of historical significance.

The wheel of the innocents

As early as 787, a Milanese priest named Dateo is said to have placed a shell outside his church to collect abandoned babies.
From 1188, the first initiatives to save such infants were organized at Chanoines hospice in Marseille (France), before Pope Innocent III (1160–1216, pontiff from 1198 until his death) institutionalized the practice.
Witnessing the terrible spectacle of the bodies of abandoned children floating on the Tiber in Rome, he planned a way to save them.
Installed at the doors of convents and designed to preserve the anonymity of desperate parents, the 'wheel of the innocents' consisted of a revolving crib accessible from the outside.
The baby was placed in the crib and a bell rung to warn the sisters who would then turn the wheel to bring it inside the convent.
Note that access to the wheel was protected by a calibrated grille that would only allow newborn babies to pass through ... This system was dropped in the 19th century but after a couple of decades had to be resurrected throughout Europe as the practice of abandoning children again became widespread.

Why are there depictions of bats throughout Barcelona?

Although many people won't ever have noticed, the Arc de Triomf, the streetlights of Passeig de Gràcia and many other iconic parts of the city show depictions of bats. For years, this little animal was a heraldic symbol included on many decorative features in the city of Barcelona, and especially on its coat of arms, as it had a mythical connection to James I the Conqueror. There are several versions of the legend, but they all focus on that monarch, and most date it to the siege of Valencia, at that time under Muslim rule.

The most detailed version tells us that, one night, while the Christian troops were resting in their camp on the outskirts of the city, a bat started to throw itself repeatedly against a war drum next to the king's tent in an attempt to wake him up. James I quickly got up and, going outside, spotted a number of enemy soldiers sneaking up under cover of darkness to ambush him and his men. Thanks to the timely warning from the winged mammal, the king raised the alarm and his troops were able to fight off the intruders. Other versions say that a bat hung itself from the roof of the monarch's tent, inside his helmet, while yet another version claims that the animal appeared inside the consecrated mosque of Palma. In every case, James I ordered the bat's life to be spared, despite it being considered an ill omen, to show that he wasn't superstitious. All versions of this story end up with James I deciding, in the light of events, to adopt the bat as his own personal symbol.

Historically, however, the bat does not appear as a symbol associated with the Spanish monarchy until the 15th century, by which time James I had already died. It started being mentioned as a symbol of the dynasty of the House of Barcelona from the time of Peter IV the Ceremonious, combined and often confused with the wyvern, a magical creature like a winged dragon that crowned (as it were) the monarch's crown.

One of the nicknames given to the wyvern from the 15th century onwards was *drac penat* (condemned dragon), which is similar to the Catalan term for bat (*rat penat*, or condemned rat), a symbolic fusing and confusing of both the name and the morphology of these two creatures.

Despite the legend of James I, the appearance of the bat as a royal symbol does not tally with the time at which he lived, though in practice it is always associated with him. After the reign of Peter the Ceremonious, the symbol did start to feature as a royal hereditary

emblem, especially in Valencia and Mallorca in the 19th century, and with the 'Renaixença' (Catalan Cultural Renaissance) and medievalist Romanticism the bat would become a popular heraldic symbol in various territories formerly ruled by James I.
For some years, the coat of arms of the city of Barcelona featured this heraldic symbol, as did the first shield of Barcelona Football Club, while it is still associated with Valencia Football Club.

Batman in Barcelona

The last time that the bat featured as a prominent symbol in the city was on 21 September 2019, but without any mention of James I or any other king, instead referring to Batman the superhero. On that day, to mark the 80th anniversary of the Caped Crusader, a great bat signal was projected over the Museu Nacional d'Art de Catalunya (National Art Museum of Catalonia: MNAC), visible across much of the city, in a synchronised link-up with other iconic buildings across the world.

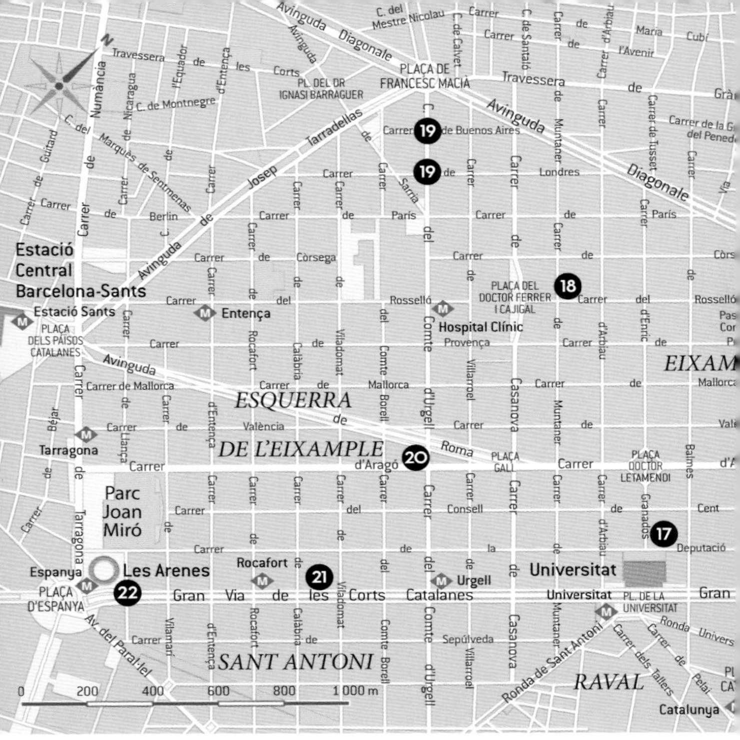

Avinguda Diagonale
C. del Mestre Nicolau
PLAÇA DE FRANCESC MACIÀ
PL. DEL DR IGNASI BARRAGUER
Travessera de les Corts
C. de Montnegre
Numància
Avinguda de Josep Tarradellas
Carrer de Buenos Aires
19
Londres
París
Còrsega
Rosselló
18
PLAÇA DEL DOCTOR FERRER I CAJIGAL
Hospital Clínic
Provença
Entença
Estació Central Barcelona-Sants
Estació Sants
PLAÇA DELS PAÏSOS CATALANES
Avinguda de Roma
Carrer de Mallorca
ESQUERRA DE L'EIXAMPLE
EIXAMPLE
València
Tarragona
Carrer d'Aragó
20
PLAÇA GALI
PLAÇA DOCTOR LETAMENDI
Parc Joan Miró
Consell de Cent
17
Deputació
Espanya
Les Arenes
22
Rocafort
21
Urgell
Universitat
PLAÇA D'ESPANYA
Gran Via de les Corts Catalanes
PL. DE LA UNIVERSITAT
Ronda Universitat
Av. del Paral·lel
Sepúlveda
SANT ANTONI
Ronda de Sant Antoni
RAVAL
Carrer dels Tallers
Catalunya
0 200 400 600 800 1 000 m

Eixample

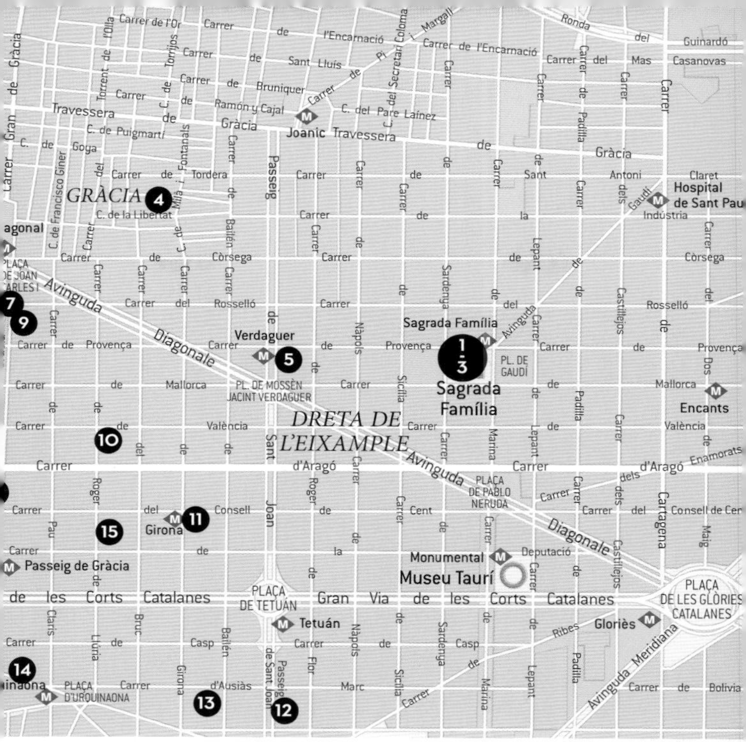
GRÀCIA
DRETA DE L'EIXAMPLE
Sagrada Família
Joanic
Verdaguer
PL. DE MOSSÈN JACINT VERDAGUER
PL. DE GAUDÍ
Hospital de Sant Pau
Encants
PLAÇA DE PABLO NERUDA
Monumental
Museu Taurí
Girona
Passeig de Gràcia
PLAÇA DE TETUÁN
Tetuán
PLAÇA DE LES GLÒRIES CATALANES
Glòries
PLAÇA D'URQUINAONA
Travessera de Gràcia
Avinguda Diagonale
Gran Via de les Corts Catalanes
Avinguda Meridiana
Passeig de Sant Joan
Carrer de Provença
Carrer de Mallorca
Carrer de València
Carrer d'Aragó
Carrer del Consell de Cent
Carrer de la Diputació
Carrer de Casp
Carrer d'Ausiàs Marc
Carrer de Rosselló
Carrer de Còrsega
Carrer de Bolivia
1-3
4
5
7
9
10
11
12
13
14
15

THE TEMPTATION OF MAN SCULPTURE ①

A diabolical weapon

Portico of the Nativity façade, Sagrada Família

Catalan society of the late 19th century was deeply divided: much of the population lived in miserable conditions while the rest accumulated vast fortunes. Some anarcho-communist workers chose a 'propaganda by deeds' strategy to denounce the dominant political, economic and social system through a terrorist campaign. Orsini bombs, a type of hand grenade designed to explode on impact, were used in various attacks.

On 24 September 1893, for example, Arsenio Martínez-Campos, Captain-General of Catalonia, was wounded by one of these bombs thrown by Paulino Pallás during a military parade at the intersection of Gran Via de les Corts Catalanes and Carrer de Muntaner. Pallás was tried and sentenced to death. When facing the firing squad, he claimed that his comrades would avenge him.

And so it was that on 7 November 1893, Santiago Salvador chose the symbolic site of the Liceu theatre to hurl two Orsini bombs from the gallery into the stalls during a performance of Rossini's *William Tell.* Mercifully the second bomb failed to detonate, falling into the lap of a woman who had already been killed. But the outcome was still terrible: twenty-two dead and thirty-five injured. Salvador took advantage of the confusion to escape, but was arrested in Zaragoza a few weeks later, in January 1894. He was taken back to Barcelona, tried, sentenced to death, and jailed in the Pati dels Corders at the Queen Amelia prison (in what is now Plaça de Josep Maria Folch i Torres, near Ronda de Sant Pau), singing the hymn to freedom, *Hijos del pueblo* (Sons of the People).

Following the Liceu outrage, part of Barcelona high society saw anarchists – and more generally the working class – as an example of the human soul at its blackest. Two years later Antoni Gaudí, a devout Christian, created a sculpture in a portico of the Nativity façade of the Sagrada Família, *La Tentación del hombre* (The Temptation of Man), showing an anarchist receiving an Orsini bomb from a demon's claws. As the proverb goes: 'Weapons are the domain of the devil.' Gaudí is emphasizing that Orsini bombs are part of that domain.

GAUDÍ'S FACE IN THE SAGRADA FAMILIA

②

A subtle tribute by Subirachs

Passion façade of the Sagrada Família – Carrer de Mallorca, 401
932 073 031 – 932 080 414 – sagradafamilia.org
Metro Sagrada Familia

On the Sagrada Familia's Passion façade, just on the left of Jesus carrying the Cross, there is a woman holding a cloth with an imprint of Christ's face. This woman, whose name is Veronica, is a reference to a relatively little-known episode from Jesus' life (see following double-page spread). On her left, we find two soldiers whose helmets are reminiscent of the chimneys of Casa Milà (La Pedrera). On their left is another figure looking at Veronica and who bears a strange resemblance

to Gaudí himself. Here Subirachs, the artist responsible for the façade, is paying a subtle tribute to the architect, depicting his face as it appears in a photo taken during the Corpus Christi procession of 11 June 1924 (see illustration). Gaudí died two years later, on 10 June 1926, having been run over by a tram.

NEARBY

The Subirachs self-portrait

On the same façade, to the right of the scene with Veronica, there is another sculptural group depicting the burial of Christ. Joseph of Arimathea (standing) and Nicodemus (kneeling at his feet) prepare to lay Christ's body in the tomb. Mary, the mother of Jesus, is pictured in between the two. The egg carved on the door above her head symbolises the future resurrection of her son. Subirachs has unwittingly given the figure of Nicodemus his own facial features in a very discreet self-portrait.

The extraordinary odyssey of Veronica's veil

In numerous churches there are depictions (often too subtle to be noticed by those not familiar with the legend) of a veil bearing the imprint of Christ's face. The origin of this image can be found in the Gospels of Mark (5:25–34), Matthew (9:20–22) and Luke (8:43–48), which tell the tale of a 'bleeding' woman (suffering from heavy menstrual bleeding) who was cured by Christ.

In about 400 CE, the Archbishop of Lydia called her Berenike, just before the apocryphal gospel of Nicodemus finally named her Veronica, although that name seems to come from the Latin 'Vera Icon' (or *eikon* in Greek), meaning 'true image', and the character of Veronica evolved gradually through the ages, finally distancing itself from the figure of the bleeding woman.

In the 7th century, another apocryphal text, the Death of Pilate, talks of Veronica as one of Christ's confidants, claiming the Messiah made her a gift of the veil with his face on it.

In about 1160, Petrus Mallius, the canon of St Peter's in Rome, came up with a hypothesis about the origins of this legend: when Christ was on his way to Golgotha, a woman had taken off her veil in order to wipe the sweat from his brow, thus leaving a miraculous imprint of the holy image.

This theory became increasingly popular until, over time, it was accepted as the true origin of this strange and mysterious *acheiropoieta* image. According to the legend, the Veil of Veronica was located in St Peter's by 1287, though Pope Clement III (1187–91) had already mentioned a shroud that may well have been Veronica's veil.

As the story goes, the veil was sold off in 1527 during the Sack of Rome. However, as is so often the case with relics, it quickly reappeared and, by the 18th century, was thought to have been rediscovered in a relic chamber, though many claimed that the face imprinted on the veil was actually that of a peasant living in a village named Manoppello. Other churches in Milan and Jaén also claim to have the true Veil of Veronica.

SAGRADA FAMILIA LABYRINTH

③

An initiatory pathway

Mallorca, 401
93 207 3031
sagradafamilia.org
November to February: Monday to Saturday 9am–6pm, Sunday 10.30am–6pm
March and October: Monday to Saturday 9am–7pm, Sunday 10.30am–7pm
April to September: Monday to Saturday 9am–8pm, Sunday 10.30am–8pm
Metro Sagrada Familia

On the Passion façade (Carrer de Sardenya, facing west) is a labyrinth sculpted in stone, next to which is a serpent whose tail is said to symbolize personal fulfilment.

The façade, also by Subirachs, has only recently been completed. In theory, it respects Gaudí's initial project, although it is difficult to be certain to what extent, because his original plans, models and sketches were destroyed during the Civil War.

On the other hand, Subirachs' work has caused great controversy as it bears little relation to Gaudí's realist style.

For more information about the symbolism of the labyrinth, see following double pages.

Labyrinths and their symbolism

In Greek mythology, one of the first labyrinths was built by Dædalus to enclose the Minotaur, a creature born of the love between Queen Pasiphæ, the wife of King Minos of Crete, and a bull. According to some archæologists, the origin of this myth may lie in the complex plans of the Palace of Minos in Knossos, Crete. Only three people were able to find their way out of the maze: the first was Theseus, who had gone to Crete to kill the beast.

Ariadne, daughter of Minos, fell in love with Theseus and gave him a ball of thread so that he could find his way out. Dædalus was also able to escape along with his son Icarus after he was imprisoned in his own labyrinth by Minos. (Some versions say that Minos wanted to prevent Dædalus revealing the plans to this labyrinth, others that Minos wanted to punish him for giving Ariadne the idea of the thread.) It turned out that Dædalus' own design for the labyrinth was so cunning that the only way for him to escape was to fly out using the wings he had made for himself and Icarus from feathers and wax.

Although the Mesopotamian, Egyptian, Hopi, and Navaho civilizations all designed and built labyrinths, there are also examples located in Europe dating from prehistory. Other

notable labyrinths built in the Christian era are to be found in the catacombs of Rome and in the churches of San Michele Maggiore in Pavia, San Savino in Plasencia, and in Lucca (Italy), as well as at Chartres and Reims (France).

These labyrinths tend to face westwards, the direction that evil spirits are said to come from (the west, where the sun sets, represents death). As these evil spirits are believed to advance in a straight line, the labyrinths are designed to trap them before they reach the churches' choir.

The relatively complex symbolism of labyrinths is also linked to the meaning of life, signifying man wandering through the universe, ignorant of where he is coming from or where he is going.

At the same time, the centre of the labyrinth represents the safe haven of divine salvation and the heavenly Jerusalem – reached only after a necessary rite of passage that may be painful and tortuous at times. The attainment of this goal is symbolized by the flight of Dædalus and Icarus, which denotes both the elevation of the spirit towards knowledge and of the soul towards God.

Ariadne's love for Theseus symbolizes love for another being, the two halves that permit an escape from the absurd human condition.

HOUSE OF THE DEVIL

A gypsy curse put on the owner out of jealousy?

Carrer de Josep Torres, 20
Metro Joanic

At No. 20 Carrer de Josep Torres, away from the more bustling parts of the popular Gràcia district, is an odd building featuring clear references to Satan, and known locally as the 'House of the Devil', though it tends to go unnoticed by the few passers-by.

The house is adorned with varying diabolical paintings, as well as reliefs of a satanic nature.

The man behind it was a manufacturer by the name of Agustí Atzeries, who over the years successfully built up a lucrative business and ordered his humble abode to be demolished and replaced by a house befitting his new social status.

To carry out the project he hired architect Joan Baptista Pons i Trabal, one of the most renowned professionals of the day, who would rise to the position of Municipal Architect.

Not much more is known about the real history of the building, but that's where popular legend takes over, explaining the reasons behind the satanic inspiration of the decorations undertaken for the 1892 renovation works.

The building is located deep in the gypsy neighbourhood. For generations the gypsies of Gràcia have made up one of the most deeply rooted communities in the history of the district, and one that has upheld the customs of this ancient and independent ethnic group that has been absorbed into the great city of Barcelona. In fact, the building stands just next to Plaça de Gato Pérez, one of the fathers of Catalan rumba.

For centuries gypsies (particularly women) have been said to have the gift of telling the future and giving blessings, although their magic is also thought to lend itself to the dark arts.

According to local legend, Atzeries' business began to fail due to a gypsy curse put on him out of jealousy. He started going bankrupt just as he was building his new and lavish house, so he promised his soul to the Devil in return for being allowed to finish the home of his dreams.

It's said his pledge was so successful that he won the lottery and, to thank Satan, he dedicated his house to him.

The building was recently renovated, and now the Devil shines in all his splendour in the sculptures and illustrations on the façade.

THE CYCLIST OF CASA MACAYA ⑤

Barcelona on two wheels

Passeig de Sant Joan, 108
Metro Verdaguer

Casa Macaya (Macaya house), now an exhibition centre for La Caixa bank, is the work of the great Catalan Modernist master, Josep Puig i Cadafalch (1867–1956).

As a pupil of Lluís Doménech i Montaner, he is considered to be the last representative of Modernism and the first of Novecentismo (a movement seeking to renew standards while reaffirming classical values).

Casa Macaya, built in 1901, offers a superb homage to the bicycle, the most practical and rapid means of transport at the time.

On the capital of one of the columns, Eusebi Arnau sculpted a bicycle. There is a woman astride it, as Arnau wanted to leave evidence of how important cycling had been in giving women freedom of movement and therefore independence.

Although the bicycle is less important today, a network of cycle lanes has been in existence since 1989, the first of which was in Avigunda Diagonal.

The artist Ramón Casas was himself a great cyclist. Casas and his friend Pere Romeu were the owners of the renowned tavern Els Quatre Gats at 3 Carrer Montsió, where there hangs a reproduction of a famous Casas painting of him and Romeu astride a tandem. The original painting is in Barcelona's Museum of Modern Art.

NEARBY

Garden of Palau Robert

Passeig de Gràcia, 107
93 238 4010
Metro Diagonal

At the junction of the busy Diagonal and Passeig de Gràcia is Palau Robert, a centre providing tourists with all kinds of information on Spain. Few know that this late 19th-century mansion has a wonderful garden where you can rest, read, or simply just enjoy the agreeable surroundings. The palace was the private home of the aristocrat Robert i Suris, who commissioned French architect Henry Grandpierre to build him a neoclassical residence.

THE DARK *PANOTS* ON PASSEIG DE GRÀCIA

⑦

Marking the shade of a holm oak that stood here in 1903

Passeig de Gràcia, 103
Metro Diagonal

On the pavement on the west side of Passeig de Gràcia, between Carrer Rosselló and Diagonal, you'll find a number of *panots* (slabs made of grey hydraulic cement) that are darker than the rest. You might well imagine that the difference in tone is due to their varying ages, but that's not quite it. What we're seeing here is the result of an initiative to reclaim little episodes from the city's history – these *panots* were laid to mark the shade of a holm oak that stood here in 1903, one of just two surviving remnants of the forest that once stretched from the centre of the city to the Vila de Gràcia before the urban development of Eixample.

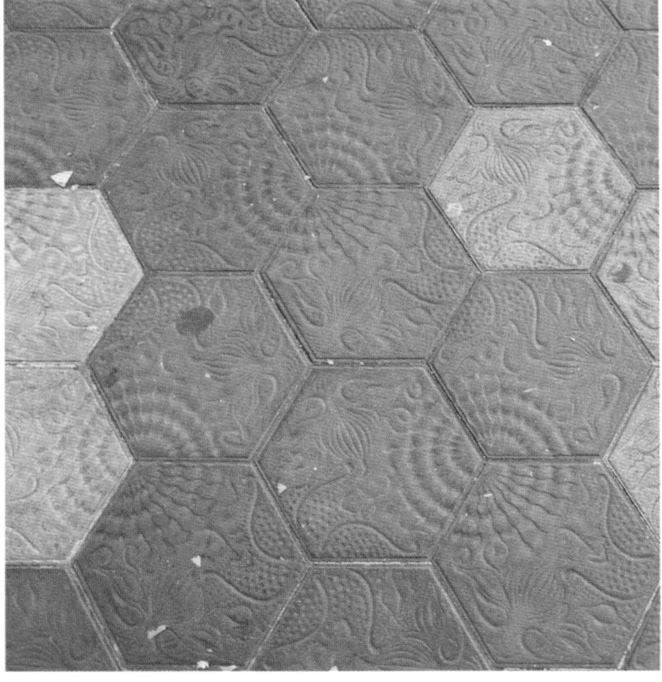

In 1908, however, by order of the City Council, the tree was cut down because it was supposedly getting in the way of the tram route. A new holm oak now stands in its place.

The old tree was immortalised by the poet and priest Jacinto Verdaguer in *A l'alzina del Passeig de Gràcia* (To the Holm Oak on Passeig de Gràcia), which refers to the relationship between nature and man; the great urban metropolis of the present and the rural world of the past.

The other holm oak stands in front of No. 24 Passeig de Gràcia.

From the time of the urban planning of Eixample (in about 1850) until it was completely developed, the district's pavements were laid haphazardly through private initiatives and funding, leading to aesthetic and practical mayhem. During the rainy seasons, the area was transformed into a muddy quagmire which was often the butt of jokes in comic strips in the satirical magazine *L'Esquella de la Torratxa*. Angry at the muddy quagmire that resulted from the rains of 1903, the citizens rose up and demanded measures be taken. That led to a public call for tenders in 1906. Various *panot* designs (including one by Gaudí) were approved, and harmonious mosaic patterns that were also waterproof were installed. Nowadays these Modernist paving slabs cover some 5 million square metres.

Blue panots

In addition to the original grey slabs, Passeig de Gràcia also boasts hexagonal blue *panots* with inverted relief. If the former (grey) ones correspond to Gaudí's original design, the latter are a reinterpretation of it from 1977. Such was the public indignation when these blue *panots* were unveiled (seen as a desecration of the Gaudí originals) that many of them were ripped up and nowadays they can only be found in specific places used to mark parking spaces.

JOSEP GUARDIOLA'S INITIALS

8

Smell the coffee at La Pedrera

Passatge de la Concepció, 4

Near Casa Milà (La Pedrera), carved over the door of No. 4 Passatge de la Concepción, the initials JG are a discreet reminder that Josep Guardiola, a businessman who was wealthy enough to commission one of Gaudí's most famous buildings, once lived here.

Josep Guardiola i Grau (1831–1901) left L'Aleixar in Tarragona, where he was born, when he was only 17. By the time he returned to Europe forty years later he had amassed a fortune of 20 million pesetas, largely through Guatemalan coffee. He had indeed spent all that time in Guatemala, specifically at San Pablo Jocopilas where he bought a property, El Chocolá, in the mid-19th century. There he managed to produce one of the best coffees in Central America, supplying the most exclusive clientele. He was also astute enough to sell the property for a thousand times more than he paid for it, before the international price of coffee fell. On moving to Paris, he began to enjoy life in the company of Roser Segimon i Artells (1870–1964), a girl from Reus who became his wife in 1891.

Every time they went to Barcelona, Josep and Roser stayed at their house in Pasaje de la Concepción, which has since become a university residence.

In 1903 the widowed Roser, still in mourning, was staying at the spa town of Vichy. Pere Milà i Camps (1874–1940), a young man of the Barcelona bourgeoisie with a reputation as a womanizer, noticed her. Two years later they were married. People were quick to point out that *Perico*, as Milà was known, had not married Guardiola's widow, but the widow's *guardiola* (piggy bank). Milà invested part of Guardiola's fortune in building a new house for the couple, Casa Milà, today one of Barcelona's best-known buildings.

NEARBY

Garden of the Ramon Casas house ⑨

The Modernist house of the Catalan Spanish artist Ramon Casas i Carbó, designed by the architect Antoni Rovira i Rabasa (1899), stands at No. 96 Passeig de Gràcia. Although the painter owned the building and lived in the main part of the house, another leading Catalan exponent of Modernism, Santiago Rusiñol i Prats, also lived here, as indicated on a plate near the door. To see what remains of Casas' home, go into the Vinçon shop and climb the stairs to admire the fireplace, garden and interior courtyard with its skylights.

ADVERTISEMENT FOR THE ANÍS DEL MONO ⑩

Delicatessen Queviures Murria

Roger de Llúria, 85
93 215 5789
Tuesday to Saturday 10am–2pm and 5pm–8pm, closed on Sunday and Monday
Metro Passeig de Gracia

Filled with exquisite and often exclusive culinary treats, the shop window of the 100-year-old delicatessen, Queviures Múrria, displays a reproduction of a poster designed by Ramón Casas, a Modernist painter who was well known in Barcelona for his graphic designs. This poster was commissioned for the liquor *Anís del Mono* (The Monkey's Anise) and although it is not the original picture, which is in the private collection of the Osborne family, it is valuable none the less.

In 1898, Ramón Casas won a competition sponsored by the Bosch distilleries in Barcelona.

The winner would go down in history by immortalizing the Anís del Mono logo. Casas found his inspiration from the stir caused by Darwin with *On the Origin of Species*, published in 1859. He interpreted Darwin's theory – that man is descended from the ape – in a rather haphazard but effective manner, and wrote on the label: 'It's the best. Science says so and I don't lie.' Casas won the competition, and Anís del Mono became an unprecedented success, which other liquor brands have tried in vain to emulate.

Queviures Múrria is a legendary store. It opened in 1898 as a coffee roaster and biscuit factory. In those days it was called La Purísima, taking its name from a nearby church.

The church that changed neighbourhood

The church of the Conception has not always stood at No. 295 Carrer d'Aragó. It used to be in Carrer de Jonqueres, but was dismantled brick by brick in 1869 and transferred to its new home. The move and reconstruction, supervised by Jeroni Granelli i Mundet, began on 29 June and took two years to complete.
Originally built in the 14th century, this Gothic church had formed part of the monastery of Jonqueres, until the municipality reclaimed the plot of land for urban development. The parishioners succeeded in having the church moved onto unbuilt land with only trees and meadows at the time, but which later became part of the Eixample. In 1879, a bell tower was added from the San Miguel church, which had also been demolished.

Iglesia de la Concepción - Aragó, 295
93 457 6552
Monday to Friday 7.30am–1pm and 5pm–9pm (entry via the cloister of carrer de Roger de Llúria,70); Saturday and Sunday 7.30am–2pm and 5pm–9pm
Metro Girona

BULLET HOLE AT No. 70 CARRER GIRONA

(11)

The traces of a gunfight between Puig i Antich and the police

Carrer Girona, 70 - Metro Girona

Through the glass at the entrance to No. 70 Carrer Girona you can see a bullet hole in one of the marble steps on the building's staircase.

This was the 1973 setting for a major gunfight between a young member of an armed Anti-Francoist group and the regime's police force.

The altercation started in the funicular bar, just on the corner. That day, Xavier Garriga, a member of the Movimiento Ibérico de Liberación (Iberian Liberation Movement) was meeting one of his cohorts, Santi Soler. Salvador Puig i Antich joined them at the last minute.

Xavier Garriga had been arrested by the police not long before and tortured. That day he was being used as bait to catch his fellow members.

As soon as they entered the bar, Santi and Salvador became suspicious of the nervous state of their comrade, Xavier, and tried to make their escape. That signalled the start of a gunfight that carried on outside the bar. The concierge at No. 70 Carrer Girona then opened the door to see what was going on.

Just then, Garriga, Salvador and the police officers entered the building, where Santi was immediately overpowered. But just when it looked like Salvador was on the ground unarmed and immobilized, he managed get free and took out a second gun, intensifying the confused gunfire.

These events resulted in the death of police officer Francisco Anguas Barragán and Salvador Puig i Antich being seriously wounded.

The doctors who first tended to the two gunshot victims still claim that the officer's body presented more bullet holes than the ones that appeared in the autopsy carried out by a military medical examiner at the police station.

Salvador Puig i Antich's court case was undertaken with few legal guarantees, and although the lawyers requested a second autopsy and a ballistic report, this was always denied.

On 2 March 1974, Salvador Puig i Antich was executed in Barcelona's Modelo prison by the 'Garrote Vil' method of strangulation.

This antiquated form of execution, which was as rudimentary as it was cruel, involved the use of an iron collar that was tightened using a nut and bolt, leading to death by either asphyxia or the breaking of vertebras and the spinal cord.

His execution caused an international outcry and large-scale anti-Franco demonstrations.

The day that Puig i Antich was killed also marked the execution in Tarragona of Georg Michael, an East German national accused of killing Civil Guard officers.

Salvador Puig i Antich and Georg Michael were the two last victims to die by Garrote Vil as ordered by the Spanish State. Although firing squad executions continued until September 1975, the death penalty was finally abolished with the 1978 Constitution.

ARÚS PUBLIC LIBRARY

⑫

Everything you always wanted to know about ...

Passeig de Sant Joan, 26 principal
93 232 2404 – bpa.es
Monday, Wednesday and Friday 10am–3pm; Tuesday and Thursday 3.30pm–8pm
Free admission for students on presentation of ID
Metro Arc de Triomf

Everything about the Arús Library is distinctive – from the luminous and pleasant entrance to the coloured marble staircase and the word 'Salve' engraved there to greet visitors. No specific style defines the place. The first impression, however, is a mysterious lack of proportion, with the rooms and their objects somehow seeming either too large or too small.

Before it was made a library, this was the private residence of Rossend Arús, a philanthropist, playwright, and masonic Grand Master, who believed that the only path to redemption was through knowledge. He died young (1847–1891) and his great legacy was this eccentric home with its extensive library on freemasonry, anarchy, and contemporary social movements.

All his life Arús thoroughly documented what was happening around him in notebooks that can be consulted in the library. The writings show his attempts to free freemasonry from any religious influence and to abandon the rituals that linked the masons with esotericism.

Founded in 1895, the library is crammed with curious details. At the top of the central staircase hangs a commemorative plaque in recognition of Arús' masonic work as Grand Master of the Regional Symbolic Grand Lodge.

Next to the plaque are Ionic columns and decorative borders painted with ancient Greek patterns, leading to a 2-metre replica of the Statue of Liberty, further underlining Arús' belief that the path to freedom is through enlightenment.

Arús himself is depicted in a portrait prominently displayed in the library, and by a bust near the exit.

The heir to a family fortune, he was bald, sported a moustache and was very elegant in his frockcoat.

He also wrote several plays. Visitors to the library can benefit from this inspiring place with its memories of Aeschylus, Poe and the other great authors he admired.

THE STONE TREES IN CASA ANTÒNIA BURÉS

(13)

A reference to mulberry trees and the silk textile industry

Ausiàs Marc, 42–46
Metro Tetuán

Commissioned from Antoni Gaudí by Antònia Burés i Borràs (whose initials you can see on the lintel over the entrance) and her husband, the textile industrialist Llogarri Torrens i Serra, the house is a fine example of Barcelona's Modernism. Its origins only came to light in 1992, almost a hundred years after it was built.

At street level, it's easy to miss the two magnificent stone trees holding up the first-floor balconies. Two rough trunks rise up out of the ground and, on reaching the balconies, are crowned by two splendid treetops, one featuring a squirrel and the other a dove.

When he received the commission, Gaudí passed the project on to a colleague of his, the architect Juli Batllevell, in recognition of the latter's help with work on Parc Güell, Casa Trias and Casa Calvet. That explains why it was Batllevell who signed the building plans, though they do have decorative and architectural features seen in works by Gaudí.

However, from the time it was built until recently, the building was not attributed to either Gaudí or Batllevell, but instead to Enric Pi, the project's contractor, who was not an architect but an associate and close friend of Batllevell (the latter was best man at his wedding). Due to this false attribution, the stone-sculpted trees holding up the balconies were also interpreted as being pines, in reference to their supposed author, as the Pi from Enric's surname means pine in Catalan.

However, the Torrens family always argued that the trees were not pines, but mulberries and that, as such, they did not refer to Enric Pi but to the family's links to the textile industry, given that mulberry leaves are the staple diet of silkworms. In fact, the morphology of the sculpted fruits would appear to support this theory.

With a bit of luck, if you arrive at the same time as the postman, you might be able to catch a glimpse of the magnificent hall and Modernist lift.

For more information about Modernism, see the following double pages.

'Modernisme' (Art Nouveau) in Catalonia

The Art Nouveau style began to make its mark in Europe from 1880 onwards and as nationalist sentiment in Catalonia strengthened and drew closer to European rather than Spanish trends, Catalans quite naturally began to adopt 'Modernisme', as it was referred to in Barcelona.

In architecture, Gaudí, Puig i Cadafalch, and Doménech i Montaner took the lead in making use of Art Nouveau's æsthetic freedom to create new forms based on nature and revamp traditional techniques. In painting, the best-known representatives of the movement were Ramón Casas, Santiago Rusiñol, and Isidre Nonell, who habitually met at the Els Quatre Gats café (Carrer de Montsió, 3), which was also frequented by Picasso, whose work of his Blue and Rose periods is considered to belong to this movement.

The name 'Art Nouveau' was popularized by Samuel Bing (1838–1905), from Hamburg, who in 1895 opened an art gallery in Paris, called *L'Art Nouveau*, where he exhibited the works of most of the major practitioners of this new art form.

The term *Jugendstil*, used today to describe a particularly geometric tendency, was the original name given to Art Nouveau in Germany and Austria.

A German publisher, George Hirth, launched the satirical review *Jugend* in Munich in 1896. Its provocative style and original typography were immediately associated with the numerous artistic novelties of the period.

Yet other terms were used to evoke Art Nouveau in Europe: *Sezessionstil*, in Austria, designated the Vienna Sezession (separatist) movement launched by Gustav Klimt in 1897. *Stile Liberty* owed its name to Liberty of London, a leading manufacturer of printed textiles, and this word was taken up mainly in Italy and the United Kingdom. Other, less-flattering names, such as *Style Nouille* (noodle style) were used by its detractors.

More than a simple artistic movement, Art Nouveau saw itself as a new mode of thinking, a new way of life, breaking with a model of society that it had rejected. It aspired to emancipate itself from the model of exploitation of working people, the role of the Church and of women, through the discovery of an eroticism and sensuality until then forbidden. Hence the many stylized representations of women's heads on the façades of buildings. The golden age of Art Nouveau in Barcelona was between 1880 and 1930.

In the rest of Europe, it suddenly disappeared after the disruption of the First World War, since it was incapable of producing buildings on a mass scale, yet limited budget. It could not therefore respond to the immense reconstruction needs of the postwar period. In Barcelona, however, the style remained vigorous and there began one of its most fertile periods in artistic terms.

HIDDEN SYMBOLS IN CASA CALVET

⑭

A direct tribute to a textile producer

Carrer de Casp, 48
Metro Urquinaona and Tetuán

The widow of the successful textile producer Pere Màrtir Calvet commissioned Gaudí to build this house. Casa Calvet features a plethora of details and discreet symbols referring to Calvet himself, to his Christian faith and his industrial activities. The letter 'C' over the entrance to the house is the initial of his surname. The door itself, meanwhile, is flanked by five columns shaped like thread bobbins, a clear allusion to the magnate's professional activities, while the door knocker is made up of a Greek cross (with four equal arms) striking the figure of a bedbug, a little blood-sucking parasite representing sin: this symbolises the Cross of Christ crushing evil every time anyone knocks at the door. The knocker ensemble is completed with the four bars from the Catalan coat of arms.

The main first-floor balcony looking over the entrance is packed with meaning: the carved cypress tree symbolises hospitality; interlinking olive branches stand for peace; the iron railing depicts different classes of fungus, a nod to Calvet's great love of mycology; a bunch of flowers on the frieze alludes to joy, and the sprigs of oak and laurel are probably a reference to nobility.

Success (that of Calvet's business) is represented by two horns replete with pears and apples, while family love is symbolised by two enamoured turtledoves.

Completing the façade we find three inverted lobe shapes and two more sticking out towards the heavens, the latter crowned by an iron cross. Underneath each of the inverted lobes are three busts, one depicting Calvet's saint's name (St Peter the Martyr) and the others representing the patron saints of the town where he was born, Vilassar de Dalt (Sts Genesius of Arles and Genesius of Rome).

Gaudí's only prize

In 1900 Barcelona City Council awarded Gaudí first prize for the best building of the year, the only award given him during his lifetime.

Casa Calvet accommodated the famous fabric business on the ground floor and in the basement, with living quarters on the upper floors.

GARDEN OF TORRE DE LAS AGUAS

15

An oasis in the city

Roger de Llúria, 56
November–March 10am–7pm; April–October 10am–9pm (approximate closing time depending on sunset)
Metro Girona

The gardens of Torre de las Aguas are a green oasis in the heart of the Eixample ('Extension') district. A wrought-iron gate, designed by Robert Llimós and decorated with undulating waves, welcomes visitors

© Jordi Domènech

into this relaxing place. The idea of setting such havens of peace amidst residential blocks originated with Ildefons Cerdà, the engineer who masterminded the Eixample expansion. In fact, the gardens of Torre de las Aguas are one of the few places that survived intact from his original plans. The magnificent and imposing tower formerly provided the neighbourhood with water, hence its name, and it is still a meeting point for local residents. Erected by architect Josep Oriol Mestres and engineer Antoní Darder in 1870, the tower presides over a small pool that is very popular with children in summer.

MUSEU DEL PERFUM

16

A museum in the back shop

Passeig de Gràcia, 39
93 216 0121
museudelperfum.com
Monday to Friday 10am–8pm, Saturday 11am–2pm
Metro Passeig de Gràcia

There is nothing outside or inside the building at No. 39 Passeig de Gràcia to indicate that this place is any different to hundreds of other modern perfumeries.

However, ask any assistant about the Perfume Museum and they will point out a door at the rear of the shop.

The moment the assistant turns on the lights, there is usually a gasp of admiration upon seeing the display cabinets which some 5,000 perfume bottles, all arranged in chronological order, beginning with censers, perfume burners, and flasks from the ancient civilizations of Egypt, Etruria, Rome and Greece. These relics are the first stop on a comprehensive tour of the history of perfumes, which also includes miniatures, catalogues, and past advertisements and perfume labels.

The museum, open since 1961, holds an extraordinary collection of perfume containers, notable both for their originality and their origins, such as the bottle that once belonged to the French queen, Marie-Antoinette.

The story behind some of the perfumes is also revealed, such as '4711,' one of the oldest brands, whose name derives from when Napoleon ordered his troops to number every house in Cologne (Germany), and 4711 Glockengasse was the house of a perfume-maker…

There are collectors' items such as the bottle Christian Dior had made in 1947 for the anniversary of Miss Dior. A limited edition of one hundred bottles was made in Baccarat crystal. There is also a bottle designed by Salvador Dalí for Le Roy Soleil perfume.

BARCELONA SEMINARY'S MUSEUM OF GEOLOGY

(17)

More than just a pile of stones

Diputació, 231
93 454 1600
On working days 4pm–6pm; it is advised to plan the visit and confirm opening hours during summer months
Free entry
Metro Universitat

Located within the Barcelona Seminary, the Geological Museum is an astonishing place where all the guides, directors, and researchers are Catholic priests.

Despite its tricky access through a maze of corridors and staircases, you should eventually find the museum entrance.

Founded in 1874, the museum specializes in palaeontology, with particular emphasis on invertebrate fossils.

It belongs to the Church of Barcelona and contains over 60,000 items dating from all geological eras.

All of the fossils are of great interest, and a guide who is both a priest and a scientist will explain how and why they preserve the remains of a prehistoric monster found in Sabadell, or why a jaw belonging to a hominid from the Miocene epoch is so valuable.

There is also a library with over 13,000 specialized volumes, and a laboratory for analysing and classifying fossils. Each year the museum publishes its own magazine, *Batallería*, where activities and new findings are described.

Most visitors are palæontology students and specialists. The priests complain that not many children visit the centre, probably because fossils do not have any gadgets or buttons to play with. In any case, it is advisable to ring before you would like to visit.

If you do get lost on the way to the museum, don't worry, you can always relax on the building's magnificent patios and balconies.

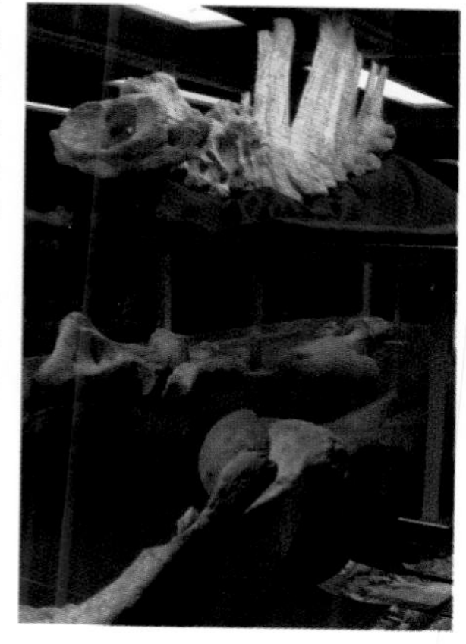

SCHOOL OF SAN MIGUEL DEL SAGRADO CORAZÓN

18

Stone by stone ...

Rosselló, 175
93 410 4005
The cloister is closed to the public, but you can make an appointment to visit or request a visit from the porter
Metro Hospital Clinic

Saint Michael of the Sacred Heart school is the unexpected home of a three-wing cloister (in the original plan there were four, but one was never built), which was transferred stone by stone from the Raval neighbourhood.

The cloister dates from the 15th century and not only has it suffered dismantling but also a fire during Barcelona's 'Tragic Week' (Setmana Tràgica) of church burnings in 1909.

Now its gargoyles are at rest in far more peaceful surroundings, watching benevolently over the basketball games of the schoolchildren.

The reason for the move was the redevelopment of Barcelona's historic city centre two decades ago, in which some buildings and monuments were replaced by public spaces.

The convent of Santa María de Jerusalem, in Plaça de la Gardunya, was one of the victims of this renovation. Its original site is now the car park of the Boqueria market, and what remained of the cloister was moved to the school.

Pulling down and moving out ...

Other convents and religious buildings suffered a similar fate. In the 19th century, another great wave of reform within the city's old quarters affected many ecclesiastical properties. At the time, the Church owned close to 20% of the urban area including cemeteries, schools, churches and convents. What was not destroyed in the burning of convents that took place in 1835 and again during the 'Tragic Week' of 1909 was expropriated by the city authorities through aggressive legal action. The transfer of the cloister of San Miguel del Sagrado Corazón is only one example of the metamorphosis that Barcelona has undergone in the past two centuries.

The most regrettable loss was the church and convent of Carme, sacrificed in order to widen Carrer dels Angels and give access to Notariat and Doctor Dou streets. The Liceu opera house was built on the former site of the convent of la Mare de Déu de la Bona Nova, while the Orient hotel in La Rambla is located on land that once belonged to the Franciscan college of Sant Bonaventura. The hotel has integrated part of the cloister into its dining area, where some blind arches can still be seen. The kitchen garden of the convent of San Agustí Vell has been turned into a square, and its library became part of the former Odeon theatre.

THE COMTE D'URGELL TRAFFIC LIGHTS

(19)

Designer traffic lights

Carrer del Comte d'Urgell
One at the junction with Carrer de Buenos Aires and another at the junction with Carrer de Londres

These silver-painted traffic lights on Carrer del Comte d'Urgell have become a symbol of bygone Barcelona. They are the oldest in town, and although nobody is quite sure of the exact date, it is believed they have been set up here since the late 1940s or early 1950s.

The lights are anchored in a block of stone and, to add to their charm, are crowned by a streetlight.

Barcelona's first traffic lights date from the Universal Exposition of 1929, and stood at the junction of Carrer de Provença and Carrer de Balmes. These early examples had to be lit manually by traffic wardens.

In later models the light would change when the passage of vehicles activated a rubber device.

During the Civil War, traffic lights were placed at Gran Vía, Plaça de Catalunya, Portal de l'Àngel, Passeig de Gràcia, Rambla de Catalunya, and Avinguda Diagonal.

AGRUPACIÓ ASTRONÒMICA DE BARCELONA (ASTER)

For stargazers

Viladomat, 291, 6.º, 1.ª
93 451 4488
669 452 024
aster.cat
Tuesday and Thursday 7pm–9pm
Metro Urgell

Set up in 1948, Barcelona's Astronomical Association (ASTER) is a select club for those devoted to stars, black holes, comets, and anything else relating to astronomy.

During the 1960s, ASTER members were the first Europeans to tune into the signal emitted by Sputnik 1, employing fairly basic techniques. Since then, the association has acquired an extensive educational role.

One of their most popular activities is the beginners' course in astronomy, open to the public, which explains such things as how to use a telescope and orientation by the stars.

The course includes fieldwork visits to the Tibidabo hillside where you can locate and name the brightest stars.

Venus, Mars, and Jupiter can be seen, and on a clear night 3,000 of the billions of stars in our galaxy can be observed. These night-time excursions last from four to five hours.

There are also daytime excursions to observe the Sun (always carried out with eye-protection equipment).

Students also learn about astrophotography, and will get the chance to take home a magnificent photograph of the moon or a starry sky.

The course costs €110, and places are limited. (The price includes a guided visit to Barcelona's Maritime Museum.)

ASTER also possesses an extensive library and newspaper archive specializing in astronomy, astrophysics, meteorology, and aeronautics, and it is the ideal place to sell or exchange telescopes, accessories, or any second-hand astronomical material.

SCULPTURES AT CASA DE LA LACTANCIA

21

Strong and healthy babies

Gran Via de les Corts Catalanes, 475
Metro Rocafort

Casa de la Lactancia (Breastfeeding House) is all that remains of a service set up in 1903 by the municipal centre for aid to pregnant women and Gota de Leche (Drop of Milk) for poor children.

The renowned contemporary sculptor Eusebi Arnau was commissioned for the lovely statues in high relief that still embellish the building. Although the central element above the main door is the most spectacular (with the sculpture of a woman bottle-feeding a baby), there is also a really charming image of a toddler suckling from a kind of gourd on top of one of the columns framing the entrance.

Casa de la Lactancia was modelled on a French centre with a mission to eradicate the micro-organisms in breast milk that could upset the stomachs of newborns. The first home of the service was in Carrer de Valldonzella, where sterilized breast milk was offered to babies to ensure their healthy development.

In 1913, the service was moved to a small villa designed by architects Antoni de Falguera and Pere Falqués. The aim was to curb the high infant mortality of the time. The centre also offered medical assistance to pregnant women and specific infant care.

The building, now a retirement home, consists of a half-basement, a ground floor and a first floor. The pretty decoration is Modernist (Art Nouveau) with a profusion of floral motifs and stained glass. The central courtyard has been covered over with a veranda.

CASA FAJOL

22

A naturalist symbol specific to Modernist aesthetic

Carrer de Llançà, 20
Residential building, the lobby is open to the public.
Metro Espanya

Popularly known as Casa de la Papallona (Butterfly House) on account of the butterfly-shaped mosaic at the top of the façade, Casa Fajol is a Modernist building commissioned by the owner, Salvio Fajol, and constructed by the architect Josep Graner between 1911 and 1929.

It comprises a ground floor and five upper storeys; there are three large windows on each of the upper floors, arranged symmetrically. The façade is characteristic of the more sober linear forms of the city's 19th-century architecture and, in accordance with Modernist aesthetic canons, has decorative elements inspired by vegetal motifs.

One of Graner's creative contributions was the building's fantastic crowning feature: a large-scale, semicircular bulging relief depicting a butterfly, covered in multicoloured (yellow, blue, green and white) ceramic mosaic, using a technique known as *trencadís*, or broken-tile mosaic.

The lobby is decorated with white/blue ceramic wainscoting imitating marble veining. The upper sections of the walls feature sgraffito work, and where they meet the ceiling there is a plaster frieze with embossed vegetal motifs framing consoles with mural paintings of Romantic inspiration.

The building stands at No. 20 Carrer de Llançà, opposite the old Las Arenas bullring, built in 1900, and next to the current Plaça de España. As such, until recently it could be seen from any part of the square, from Parc de l'Escorxador and a section of Gran Vía. However, since the 2009 conversion of Las Arenas into a shopping centre, with its adjoining modern hotel, you can only get a full view of the magnificent butterfly from Carrer de Llançà itself.

Beyond its unique quality as an architectural ornament, Graner's butterfly expresses the artistic sentiment that emerged at the turn of the 20th century: the splendour of beauty, the resurgence of life, based on the simplicity of the caterpillar and its metamorphosis. An animalistic and naturalistic symbolism that was typical of the Modernist aesthetic, with its 'internal gardens', present in both architecture and metalwork, painting and decorative elements.

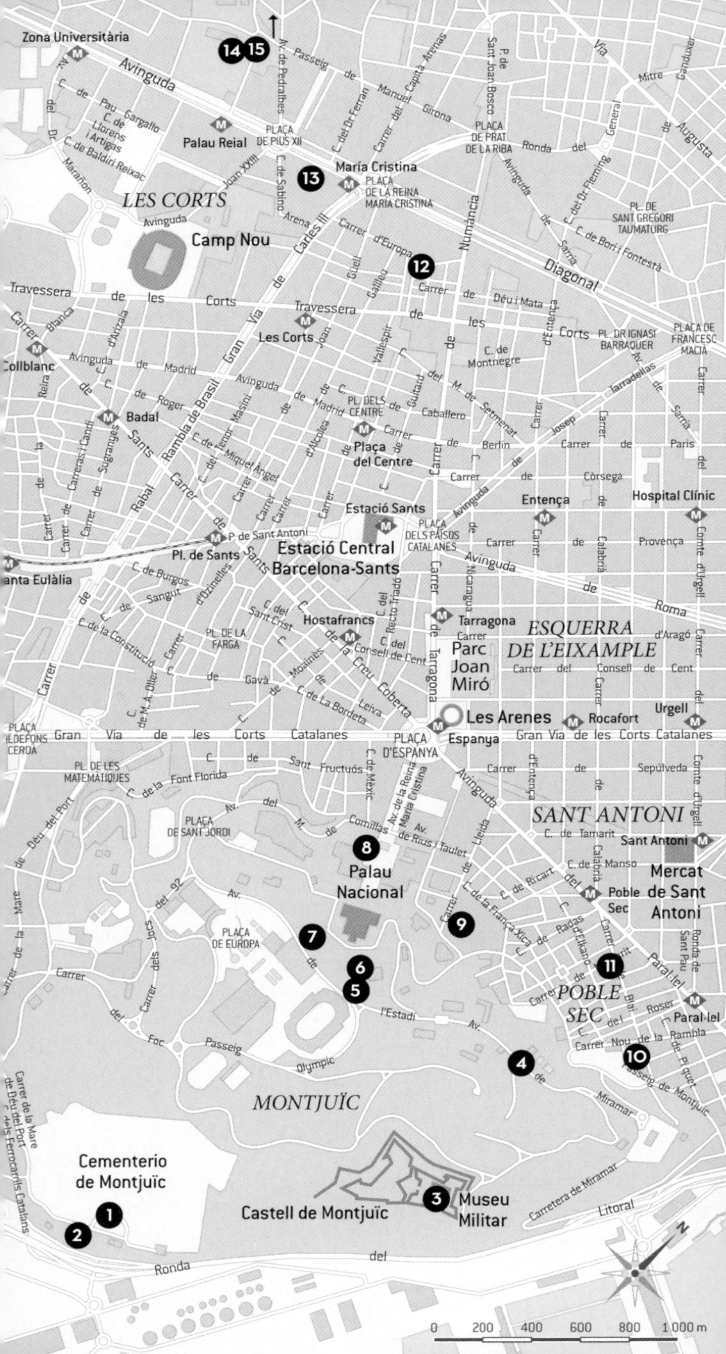

Zona Universitària
14
15
Avinguda
Palau Reial
PLAÇA DE PIUS XII
Passeig de Manuel Girona
Carrer del Capità Arenas
P. de Sant Joan Bosco
PLAÇA DE PRAT DE LA RIBA
Ronda del General Mitre
Via Augusta
Gandaxer
María Cristina
PLAÇA DE LA REINA MARIA CRISTINA
13
LES CORTS
Camp Nou
C. de Pau Gargallo
C. de Llorens i Artigas
C. de Baldiri Reixac
Av. del Dr. Marañón
Joan XXIII
C. de Sabino Arena
C. del Dr. Ferran
Carles III
Carrer d'Europa
12
Numància
Avinguda de Sarrià
C. del Dr. Fleming
PL. DE SANT GREGORI TAUMATURG
C. de Bori i Fontestà
Diagonal
Travessera de les Corts
Travessera de les Corts
Les Corts
Carrer de Déu i Mata
C. de Montnegre
PL. DR IGNASI BARRAQUER
PLAÇA DE FRANCESC MACIÀ
Güell
Galileu
Vallespir
Gran Via de Carles III
Collblanc
Carrer Blanca
Avinguda de Madrid
C. de Roger
Badal
Rambla de Brasil
C. del Tenor Masini
C. de Miquel Àngel
PL. DELS CENTRE
Caballero
M. de Setmenat
Tarradellas
Avinguda de Josep Tarradellas
Carrer de Berlín
Carrer de París
Av. de Sarrià
Carrer de Còrsega
Plaça del Centre
Carrer de Sants
Carrer de Sugranyes
Carrer de Carreras i Candi
Estació Sants
Estació Central Barcelona-Sants
PLAÇA DELS PAÏSOS CATALANS
Entença
Hospital Clínic
Carrer de Provença
P. de Sant Antoni
Pl. de Sants
Santa Eulàlia
C. de Burgos
C. de Sanguí
C. d'Ozinelles
C. del Sant Crist
Hostafrancs
C. del Recto Triadó
Avinguda de Roma
C. Nicaragua
Tarragona
Carrer de Tarragona
ESQUERRA DE L'EIXAMPLE
Carrer d'Aragó
Carrer del Consell de Cent
Carrer Comte d'Urgell
C. de la Constitució
PL. DE LA FARGA
C. del Consell de Cent
Parc Joan Miró
C. de Gavà
C. Moianès
C. de La Bordeta
Leiva
Creu Coberta
C. de M. A. Oller
Les Arenes
Rocafort
Urgell
PLAÇA ILDEFONS CERDÀ
Gran Via de les Corts Catalanes
PLAÇA D'ESPANYA
Espanya
PL. DE LES MATEMÀTIQUES
C. de Sant Fructuós
C. de la Font Florida
C. de Mèxic
Av. de la Reina Maria Cristina
Av. de Rius i Taulet
Carrer de Sepúlveda
Avinguda de Lleida
Av. del M. de Comillas
PLAÇA DE SANT JORDI
SANT ANTONI
C. de Tamarit
Sant Antoni
C. de Manso
Mercat de Sant Antoni
8
Palau Nacional
C. de Ricart
C. de la França Xica
Poble Sec
Av. de l'Estadi
9
PLAÇA DE EUROPA
7
6
5
Carrer de la Mare de Déu del Port
Carrer dels Jocs del 92
Carrer del Foc
C. de Radas
C. d'Elkano
Carrer de Blai
11
POBLE SEC
C. del Roser
Paral·lel
Carrer Nou de la Rambla
10
Passeig de Montjuïc
Carrer de Piquer
Ronda de Sant Pau
Passeig Olympic
4
Av. de Miramar
MONTJUÏC
Carrer de la Mare de Déu del Port
C. dels Ferrocarrils Catalans
Cementerio de Montjuïc
1
2
Castell de Montjuïc
3
Museu Militar
Carretera de Miramar
Litoral
Ronda del Litoral
N
0
200
400
600
800
1 000 m

West

MONTJUÏC CEMETERY

①

Occult symbolism of the Batlló family tomb

Cementerio de Montjuic
Mare de Déu del Port, 56-58
93 484 1999
Daily 8am–6pm
Bus 13 and 125

The symbolism of the tomb of the Batlló family (the most famous of whose representatives was José Batlló Casanovas, a major Barcelonian textile manufacturer in the late 19th and early 20th centuries who was also behind the famous Casa Batlló built by his close friend Gaudí) is as interesting as it is little known.

The angel of death, on a pedestal surmounting the mausoleum, carries a scythe in the left hand and holds a chalice aloft in the right. He represents the guardian of souls, who is also their guide for this last trip from Earth to Heaven, from corporal death to spiritual immortality. The scythe stands for death and pain struck down, which is why it is lowered, while the chalice shows the feeling of love that persists over time, through generations of the dead.

On each side of the entrance to the tomb, an angel is set on a column.

Seen from the front, the one on the left (male) carries the candle of spiritual resurrection – the four candles that burn around the body of the deceased (the three on the altar represent the Trinity) symbolize the purity of the spiritual flame ascending to Heaven. The halo around the head of the male angel forms the Greek letter *omega*, signifying 'the end'.

Seven stars are drawn around its inner rim: they represent the seven archangels in the Hebrew and Gnostic tradition (Michael, Gabriel, Samael, Raphael, Sariel, Haniel, Cassiel) who link man and God.

On the right a female angel holds a palm leaf, echoing the theme of resurrection of the soul. The Palm Sunday branches, like European boxwood, herald the resurrection of Christ after the tragedy of Golgotha. Incidentally, the palm of martyrdom has the same meaning, and the tradition of laying wreaths by the bodies of the deceased recalls this. The branches symbolize the certainty of the immortality of the soul and the spiritual resurrection of the dead.

At the feet of each angel is an owl, symbol of prudence (represented by the female angel) and wisdom (personified by the male angel).

On the lintel above the door of the tomb are two eagle's wings in the centre of which is a circular inscription of the chrism (Greek initials of the name of Christ, Xpô), which indicates the presence of the Spirit of Christ gathering unto him all those who pass the threshold of death.

MASS GRAVE OF 'LA PEDRERA' ②

Mass grave for unpaid coffins and unidentified bodies

South-west Montjuïc cemetery
Carrer Mare de Déu del Port, 56–58
Monday to Sunday 8am–6pm

One of the most peaceful, spacious and yet little-known places in Barcelona is the site of the mass grave where, during the Franco dictatorship, the regime buried its firing squad victims.

This is a vast and diaphanous grassy plateau protected by huge walls built with rocks extracted from the hill itself.

From Roman times until quite recently, Monjuïc was the place from which the majority of the stones used to build the city of Barcelona were sourced, whether Roman temples or Modernist buildings.

This explains why it is full of the remains of old quarries that pass unnoticed even by most of the city's residents. One of the most impressive is located at the western limits of Montjuïc cemetery.

This spot, which was previously known as Moragas quarry or, more recently, the Mass Grave of La Pedrera (Catalan for quarry), was used for a time as a burial site for people whose coffins had not been paid for, and unidentified bodies, or for those without financial means. Once the Francoist forces entered the city, its use intensified.

Modest wooden boxes arrived here carrying the bodies of those who had faced the firing squads of Modelo prison or the Camp de la Bota neighbourhood, and they were buried in quicklime to speed up their

decomposition.

Few family members arrived in time to identify their loved ones' bodies, with one example being the sister of the President of the Generalitat (Catalan government), Lluís Companys, exiled in France and handed over by the Gestapo. He faced the Montjuïc castle firing squad on 15 October 1940.

Companys was the only democratically elected president to be executed in Europe.

Although at his sister's request Companys was buried in his own niche, it was unmarked in order to avoid it becoming a pilgrim site. He was transported to the mass grave with the rest of the victims and a little mausoleum was built.

When Beth Galí designed the project to renovate the area, she included a monument to the former president, and pillars to commemorate the place with the names of many of those who were executed by the regime, some of whom are buried there.

There is also a monument to Anarchist victims, a copy of the one in front of the 'Parlament' dedicated to those who made the ultimate sacrifice for freedom in Catalonia, and another to the victims of the Nazi Holocaust, as well as a range of tombstones for specific people at the end of the mass grave: members of the International Brigade, political parties or trade unions, along with masons and others whose names have been included.

Symbolism of the trees in Montjuïc cemetery

Since it was opened, the cemetery has aspired to great aesthetic heights: many of the tombs face the sea and the choice of plants follows the principles of life and death, on the recommendations of Celestino Barallat, specialist in necrological themes and author of the unusual gardening treatise, *Principios de botánica funeraria* (Principles of Funerary Botany).

According to Barallat, some plants are appropriate to a cemetery while others counteract the principle of eternal rest. Thorny plants are banned, for example, with two exceptions: hawthorn, which is synonymous with hope, and the wild rose. Nor are cacti acceptable, although some have been allowed as a metaphor for strength in suffering. On the other hand, cypresses, the magical trees of the Celts and symbols of woodland, are often found along with green swards of lawn, as in Paradise; abundant ivy; yellow everlasting flowers, which in Christian iconography stand for revelation and the herald of eternal glory; and finally the willow, symbol of sadness.

MONUMENT TO THE METRE AT MONTJUÏC CASTLE

③

When the Montjuïc castle was used as a reference for the creation of the metre

The monument, that can't be reached since it's located in a ditch, can be seen from outside
Bus 50 and 55

In the dry moat around Montjuïc castle stands a sculpture honouring the metre. *La talla métrica de la natura* ('The metric measure of nature'), by Valérie Berjeron, is a concrete column 9 metres high, set between three trees with different rates of growth: oak, apricot and white poplar. It was sited here because the castle tower served as a reference point for the measurements carried out by Pierre-François Méchain in the 18th century.

The monument does not get many visitors – few stop to reflect on its beauty and the achievement that it commemorates.

Adventures of the metric system

Not many Barcelona residents appreciate to what extent their city was involved in the development of the metre. Nor do many suspect that avenues such as Meridiana and Paral-lel pay tribute to this unit of length, and indirectly to the 18th-century geographers, scientists, topographers, and explorers who carried out the extremely complex observations and calculations required to define it over a period of six years.

The task of making the measurements fell to two French topographers: Pierre-François Méchain and Jean-Baptiste Delambre.

Delambre was responsible for the northern part of the meridian arc, between Dunkirk and Rodez (France), while Méchain measured the section from Rodez to Barcelona.

Their 'geodesic triangulation' technique consisted of tracing a line of triangles whose apexes corresponded to the mountain peaks along the meridian.

Méchain worked in close collaboration with two mathematicians appointed by the Spanish king: José Chaix and Juan de Peñalver. For six years, Méchain and his team travelled with their extremely fragile or extremely heavy measuring instruments, erecting what came to be known as 'signal towers', often in severe weather. They were accused of spying and were almost caught up in a war.

In 1798, Méchain and Delambre met at Carcassonne before returning to Paris with their results, which, even though they were approved, failed to fully satisfy the Académie Française. So Méchain journeyed southwards again in 1802, extending the measurements as far as Ibiza in order to achieve greater accuracy in the definition of the metre.

He died from malaria in 1804 and is buried at Castellón. Researchers carried on trying to perfect the unit of length until 1983 (see p. 228).

Pierre François Méchain

Jean-Baptiste Delambre

THE JOAN BROSSA GARDENS

4

One of the most magical yet uncrowded parks in Barcelona

Plaça Danter
Monday to Sunday from 10am to dusk
Montjuïc funicular: Montjuïc Park station

The Joan Brossa Gardens are one of the most magical yet uncrowded parks in Barcelona.

The gardens were established in 2000 on the site of the old Montjuïc Parque de Atracciones (Theme Park), which finally closed its doors in 1998 after an agonizing fall from grace. The old paths going from one amusement to the next are the same ones leading to the various play areas. On the way, you'll come across various statues that once graced the park, dedicated to Charlie Rivel the clown, gymnast Joaquín Blume, Chaplin's tramp and so on.

One of the oddest features to survive the Theme Park is a great concrete construction shaped rather like a wild mushroom on a surprisingly narrow base considering the weight it supports. At one time it was seen as an architectural feat and was the focal point of Bar Fanta, sponsored by the soft drink company.

But the old park was itself a reusable structure. Bear in mind not only the fact that at the top there was once an original park called Maricel, but also that the land previously played host to a military detachment, the Álvarez de Castro company, which occupied the site from the Cuban war until 1964 when the Town Council purchased the land from the army.

Some of the park structures were recycled military facilities, and the fact is that the old 'ghost train' used the gunpowder tunnels, since blocked off and covered in ivy, for the carriages to pass through.

Montjuïc hill is actually full of military tunnels, some of which are unknown, hard to access or have simply remained unexplored for decades.

Its history lends the new park a special atmosphere, but this is particularly the case for the visual poetry of Joan Brossa, to whom the garden and original games for the little (and not so little) ones, which are scattered around it, are dedicated.

Along with musical cushions, slides and enormous spider's webs, the star attractions of the area around the old Bar Fanta are two concrete parabolic reflectors erected one in front of the other, a few metres apart.

As long as nobody interferes with the imaginary line that links them, sound reverberates in such a way that a person in one reflector can hear what a person in the other is saying, even if they whisper.

MONTJUÏC'S SECRET *MASIA* ⑤

Built for Barcelona's International Expo of 1929

Jardí Botànic Històric de Barcelona
Av. dels Montanyans, 40
Getting there: go to the back of the Palacio Nacional (MNAC headquarters) and just on the right, by the escalator with a bronze statue of Francesc Ferrer i Guàrdia at the top, you'll find a gate with a sign showing the entrance to the Jardí Botànic Històric de Barcelona (Historical Botanical Garden of Barcelona). As you go in, there are lawns you can stroll through on the right, while on the left, if you go under the arch that supports the escalator, you'll find a 'masia' surrounded by vegetable gardens
Nov–Jan 10am–5pm; Feb, March & Oct 10am–6pm; April, May & Sept 10am–7pm; June–Aug 10am–8pm. Sat mornings for children's games and workshops

Located inside the Historical Botanical Garden of Barcelona, the masia of Montjuïc is a secret place built by the architect Eduard Maria Balcells i Buïgas at the behest of the Cattle Breeders' Association for the Barcelona International Exposition of 1929.

It stands in one of the pits left by the old Foixarda quarry, just next to where the Historical Botanical Garden is today (itself a little-known spot). If Montjuïc's orography means the mountain itself is full of

hard-to-find nooks and crannies, the openings left by the quarries that for centuries supplied the city with building materials have now been transformed into a green lung with even more hidden secrets.

When it comes to building materials, these quarries were 'the lifeblood of Barcelona' from pre-Roman times right up to the early 20th century. In fact, even in the 1970s there were still stone excavations and it was not until the Olympic Games of 1992 that stone mining came to an end.

The pits, popularly known locally as 'sots' and whose activity left these scars on the mountainside, were used to install various facilities that you wouldn't know were there unless you were told.

The main idea at the time they were constructed was to build a *masia*, or large traditional rural complex in contextualised surroundings, to show city dwellers what rural life was like in Catalonia. There were other small buildings where people could buy cattle and agricultural goods.

Refurbishments were carried out in 1940 and then the site remained closed to the public from 1986 until 2003. Perhaps this long closure – together with the *masia*'s location at the foot of an old quarry pit surrounded by far more striking elements such as the Olympic Stadium or the Museu Nacional d'Art de Catalunya (National Art Museum of Catalonia: MNAC) – explains why for many people this place is both mysterious and unknown.

PALAUET ALBÉNIZ ⑥

Decoration by Dalí, tapestries designed by Goya, a hall of mirrors inspired by Versailles ...

Avinguda de l'Estadi – 93 292 42 12
Gardens: Sat & Sun 10am–3pm
Visits inside exclusively during 'La Mercè' festival (24 September)
Metro Espanya

As discreetly tucked away as it is opulently majestic, the Albéniz 'Palauet' (mansion), which belongs to Barcelona City Council and is a Spanish royal family residence, is one of the city's most aristocratic locations in Montjuïc, camouflaged between the Museu Nacional d'Art de Catalunya and Avinguda de l'Estadi.

The building and its gardens are surrounded by lookout towers, and official cars drive in and out through a gateway opposite the rear façade of the museum, leading directly to an entrance that slips inside the hillside, providing access to the palace basements.

Entry to these facilities was extremely limited until relatively recently, but nowadays the gardens can be visited on Saturday and Sunday mornings. The palace is still restricted to the royal family and select VIPs, but for the past few years a number of rooms have been open to the public on the day of 'La Mercè' festival (an opportunity not to be missed).

During the King of Spain's last visit, there was much media speculation on the possibility of the royal family staying overnight.

But what is this Bourbon/Versailles-style mansion doing here, and why was it built?

The news that a new International Expo was going to be held in Barcelona in 1929 was the trigger for a whole series of building projects aimed at urbanizing Montjuïc hill. Developments from that period include Plaça Espanya, Avinguda Maria Cristina, the Palau Nacional and Poble Españyol.

With preparations well under way, in 1923 army officer Miguel Primo de Rivera (father of the founder of the Spanish extreme right-wing Falange party, José Antonio Primo de Rivera) carried out a coup d'état with the support of the financial elites (with those from Catalonia particularly prominent, incidentally) and the monarchy, against a backdrop of major working-class unrest.

The new regime shifted the symbolism of the future Expo, ordering the demolition of four Ionic pillars designed by Puig i Cadafalch, which had been erected opposite the Fuente Mágica (Magic Fountain) to symbolize the four stripes on the Catalan flag and the roots of classical culture, and replacing the name of what was going to be Iberona with the concept of the Spanish People, or Poble Espanyol.

Given the context, it was important to reinforce the monarchy, one of the pillars of the new regime. The commission for works on the palace went to the architect Juan Moya, who followed a style drawing on the Baroque of the reign of Philip V, echoing the Escorial, Zarzuela and the royal residences of Madrid, rather than the Mediterranean architecture used in other heritage buildings.

King Alfonso XIII and Queen Victoria Eugenia did not stay at the mansion during the Expo, preferring the Palau de Pedralbes, another location built at that time on lands belonging to the count of Güell, with financial contributions from prominent monarchists in the city.

In 1934, with the arrival of the 2nd Republic, there was a suggestion that the building might be turned into a music museum, and although that idea did not bear fruit, from then on it would be known as Palauet Albéniz in homage to composer Isaac Albéniz.

The mansion remained closed for many years and, during the period when Josep Maria de Porcioles was city mayor, it was reopened for VIPs. In the 1970s the gardens were expanded and the building was renovated to include valuable elements such as the decoration by Dalí on one of the ceilings (see photo).

Even today the Palauet Albéniz houses tapestries designed by Goya and a hall of mirrors that was inspired by Versailles.

MONUMENT TO FERRER I GUÀRDIA

⑦

Free citizens of the future

Avinguda de l'Estadi (acceso al Palau Nacional)
Metro Espanya – Bus 50

In 1901, Francesc Ferrer i Guàrdia (1859–1909), a rationalist educator and freethinker, founded the Escuela Moderna (Modern School) at No. 56 Carrer de Bailén. Its aim was to produce free citizens of the future by offering a secular mixed education, regardless of social class. Ferrer i Guàrdia ended corporal punishment, insisted on the importance of children being in contact with nature and prompted them to question anything that seemed unreasonable. The Modern School soon opened branches throughout Catalonia, although objections to the project were growing meanwhile among supporters of traditional values, especially after the 1906 attempted assassination of Alfonso XIII and his bride Victoria Eugenia by Mateo Morral, a school employee.

In July 1909, during the *Setmana Tràgica**, churches and monasteries were burned down. Ferrer i Guàrdia was accused of being behind this popular uprising, although he had nothing to do with it. Despite the lack of evidence, he was imprisoned, tried and sentenced to death. The voices raised in his support throughout Europe had no effect: he was executed by firing squad at Montjuïc fortress on 13 October 1909.

Protesting his innocence, he was taken to the place of execution with his head held high and demanding not to be blindfolded … in vain. He died proclaiming, 'Long live the Modern School!' Ferrer i Guàrdia's reputation was justly, though belatedly, restored in 1990, when a replica of the Brussels monument (1911) that honoured him as a martyr to the freedom of thought was erected at Montjuïc. The bronze statue is of a naked man standing on tiptoe to proffer, with both hands, a blazing torch representing the light of rationalism. The monument is halfway between Palau Nacional and Palau Sant Jordi, near the escalator to Avinguda de l'Estadi.

**The series of confrontations from 26 July to 2 August 1909 between the army and the working class, incited by the decision to call up reserve troops to restore order in North Africa, is known as the Setmana Tràgica (Tragic Week). These uprisings took place throughout Spain but were particularly violent in Barcelona.*

In 2010, Avinguda del Marquès de Comillas was also named Avinguda de Ferrer i Guàrdia. Another gesture from Barcelona for a man who, as engraved on the pedestal, 'died to defend social justice, brotherhood and tolerance'.

VESTIGES OF THE OLD PALAU NACIONAL FUNICULAR RAILWAY

⑧

A relic from the 1929 International Expo

Corner of Passeig de Jean Forestier and Carrer de la Guàrdia Urbana
Metro Plaça Espanya

Barcelona has steadily modernized its look from one major event to another. Starting with the Universal Exposition of 1888 right the way through to the 2004 Universal Forum of Cultures, the city has always made the most of these chances to show the world its best side.

One of the traditions for this sort of event has always been to convert decaying, neglected or simply undeveloped parts of the city, and transform them into model areas. Some of the infrastructures continue to be of use afterwards while others have a more limited lifespan.

In the case of the 1929 International Expo, the area developed was Montjuïc hill in the southern part of the city.

Plaça Espanya was developed as an entrance to the Expo complex, and the Palacio Nacional (which now houses the Museu Nacional d'Art de Catalunya) was installed at the top of the hill.

Plaça Espanya became the destination of 14 tram and 12 bus routes during the Expo, although both trams and buses had great difficulty overcoming the hill's considerable ups and downs.

This resulted in a number of funicular railways and cable cars being built in the city, connecting the developed area with main parts of the hill.

Some of these are still in service, and the spooky remains of the structure of the old funicular that connected the bottom of the hill with the Palau Nacional can still be seen, hidden in the undergrowth and covered in graffiti next to a monument to Occitan poet Frédéric Mistral.

That cable car connected the old end of tram line 61 (linking Plaça Catalunya with the bottom of the hill) with the Palau Nacional. Its entire run was only 95.5 m long, but it scaled a slope measuring 28.5 metres. It had three cars which could each carry 100 passengers. In its day, this structure transported as many as 3,000 passengers an hour.

The life of the cable car was but a brief one, as it was dismantled after the International Expo, although the carriages were reused to transport passengers on the Vall de Núria funicular railway near the French border.

Nowadays, if you want to climb to the top of the hill you can either use conventional steps or the escalator that was installed during yet another major event, the 1992 Olympics.

MURAL MADE UP OF POTS AND PANS

9

A solution to an aesthetic problem

Plaça d'Ovidi Montllor – Metro Espanya

Near Plaça d'Ovidi Montllor is a narrow alleyway separating the Institut del Teatre (Theatre Institute) and the Mercat de les Flors (Flower Market), decorated with no less than 1,500 misshapen glazed ceramic pots set into the market's red-coloured wall.

This installation, the work of Barcelona artist Frederic Amat, was the solution to an aesthetic problem commissioned by the institute, which ended up impacting on the next-door building.

The institute management contacted Amat to ask him to decorate the ceiling near the glass wall that looked over the shared alleyway. The sight of a blank wall through the glass distorted the agreeable image they wanted to transmit from the institute façade.

Amat examined the situation and opted against an artistic installation on the ceiling, because he felt it was too low, instead suggesting a logical solution: if the aesthetic problem was the blank wall of the building seen through the glass, then that was where the answer lay.

In theory the idea seemed a bit farfetched, because the Mercat was council property, and one owner cannot carry out works on another property, but a three-way meeting was organized with the institute, the flower market and the town council, and Amat's concept was approved on the condition that a glass marquee was installed over the alley (which, incidentally, makes the installation less visible).

But why so many pots and pans on the wall?

Frederic Amat is a lover of agglomerations of objects. On a trip to India, he was at Jaipur market and saw a load of pots and watermelons piled up. The aesthetic of repetition fascinated him, and he took a photo as both artistic and architectural inspiration.

According to him, misshapen pots symbolize transformed heads or the piling up of skulls.

Better known is his installation on the walls of the city-centre Hotel Ohla on Via Laietana, from which something like 1,000 protruding ceramic eyeballs can be seen.

There was a plan to cover the walls of the Gran Teatre del Liceu with 170 red ceramic hoops evoking the horseshoe shape of the theatre stalls, but it came to nothing through lack of consensus.

REFUGI 307

A historic air-raid shelter

Nou de la Rambla, 169 – 93 256 2100
Guided tours on Sunday at 10:30am (in English), 11:30am (in Castellano) and 12:30pm (in Catalan), with mandatory booking
From Monday to Saturday, group visits can also be booked
Closed on bank holidays
Metro Paral-lel

Visiting one of the few remaining air-raid shelters that protected the people of Barcelona during the Civil War can be a terrifying experience. Refugi 307 is a trip back in time, to a conflict that still endures in living memory. The residents of the Poble Sec neighbourhood took refuge there from the relentless aerial bombardment waged by Mussolini's air forces.

The site was discovered by chance during Holy Week 1995, following the demolition of a glassworks that revealed one of the three entrances to the shelter.

Built in 1937, it was one of the best equipped at the time, with electricity provided by a portable generator, an infirmary, sanitary facilities, and water fountains fed by the Montjuïc springs. In theory it could protect 2,000 people from the bombing, but as construction was never finished the actual number is not known.

Over a period of two years, 1,400 shelters were built in Barcelona, 288 of which were in what is now the Sants-Montjuïc district.

Today, little remains but a few scattered ruins. The renovation of the sewer system and the construction of underground car parks saw the end of most of these shelters. Refugi 307 is one of the rare examples to have survived urban development.

It was also the only shelter not to be closed down by Franco's troops. After the war it was used for growing mushrooms, as storage space for a glassworks, and as a shelter for the homeless. It was closed from the 1960s until its rediscovery in 1995.

Today you can visit the shelter accompanied by a guide who explains the main events of the Civil War and the efforts the citizens made to create havens where they would be safe from the terror of the bombs.

Other air-raid shelters

Of the 1,400 air-raid shelters known to have existed during the Civil War, only a few have survived. Most were buried and rediscovered during development work or the extension of the metro.

One of these shelters, at Plaça del Diamant, is a network of tunnels with a sickbay and sanitary facilities. Discovered in 1992 during the renewal of an electricity plant, it is one of eighty-eight shelters in the Gràcia neighbourhood.

Work on a new car park at Plaça de la Revolución brought to light another air-raid shelter. It proved impossible to save it intact and only the sickbay and part of the corridor could be recovered. The narrow entrance is by a door within the car park.

In the Caollserola foothills, a millionaire businessman had built a residence named Palau de les Heures. The house stood empty after he died in 1898 until the Generalitat (the autonomous government of Catalonia under the Spanish Republic) took it over during the Civil War. Its shelter is perfectly preserved.

The bunker of the former Soviet consulate, in Carrer del Tibidabo, 17–19, is also complete. Inside its concrete walls are several offices, a kitchen, and sleeping quarters, all protected by two armoured doors that can be opened and closed only from the inside. Another private shelter was built in Gaudí's famous Casa Milá. Members of

the Unified Socialist Party of Catalonia (PSUC, Partit Socialista Unificat de Catalunya) took refuge there. It was demolished in renovation work in 2000.
A manhole cover in Plaça de Tetuán serves as the entrance to another shelter that remains in an excellent state of conservation. Also worth a look is No. 6 Carrer de la Fusina, where the sturdy building, now a bar, was an attractive neighbourhood shelter.
Other shelters can be found at Can Peguera, at Carrer de Sardenya near the Sagrada Família, and the one at Avingunda de Pedralbes, used by the President of the Spanish Republic, Juan Negrín, when he resided in Barcelona.
Although these shelters are in excellent condition, not all of them are open to visitors, unless they have special permission.
Many of them are quite hazardous, and can only be entered with ropes and potholing equipment.

To visit the Plaça del Diamant shelter:
Ajuntament de Gràcia: 93 211 4973

To visit the Palau de les Heures shelter:
Fundación Bosch i Gimpera: 93 403 9100

PLAQUE MARKING THE HOUSE OF FRANCESC BOIX

(11)

The fantastic story of the photographer who helped convict the Nazis running Mauthausen and Dachau

Carrer Margarit, 17
Metro Poble Sec or Paral·lel

At No. 17 Carrer Margarit in the Poble Sec district, a plaque embedded in a paving stone bears witness to the fact that this was the house where Francesc Boix was born. Boix was a young photographer who, while a prisoner in the Nazi camp of Mauthausen, managed to conceal the negatives of photos that would later serve to help convict leading Nazis from both Mauthausen and Dachau at the Nuremberg trials.

Born in 1920, Francesc Boix was introduced to the world of photography by his father, a tailor and camera afficionado. After the Civil War broke out, the 17-year-old Francesc enlisted as a photographer for the Republicans' 30th Division. When they lost the war, he escaped into France along with thousands of other Spanish Republicans, where they settled in refugee camps. When these camps were disbanded at the outbreak of the Second World War, the refugees were given two options: go back to Franco's Spain or work and/or fight alongside the French Republic. Boix joined a battalion of foreign workers and ended up being captured by the Nazis.

The Francoist government was consulted by the National Socialist authorities regarding what to do with any captured Spanish citizens who were opposed to Franco's regime. They chose to wash their hands of them, leaving them stateless … meaning that they were taken to the Third Reich's concentration camps.

Francesc Boix was imprisoned in Mauthausen (Austria), where his skills with a camera saved him from the harsher details as he was appointed to photographic duties. Risking his own life, and with the help of other prisoners, he devoted himself to hiding the negatives of photographs of the atrocities committed by the officers in charge of the camp, so these could be used as damning evidence at some point in the future.

Following their defeat at Stalingrad, and aware they were losing the war, the Nazis wanted to destroy all evidence of their crimes. But they did not know about the negatives that Boix was hiding. With the help of prisoners who left the camp each day to work outside, some of the negatives were hidden in the wall of a house belonging to a local woman who was sympathetic to the Resistance.

That was how, once he had been liberated by US troops on 5 May 1945, Francesc Boix, who had survived the horror, was able to give his own personal testimony and, with the irrefutable proof of his photographs, convict his jailors.

In May 2022 a *stolpersteine* was fitted to mark his house. Literally meaning 'stumblestone', these now identify many of the places in Europe where victims of Nazism were born.

MODERNIST MOSAIC AT CRISTALLERIES PLANELL 12

The scene of a bitter children's strike

Centre Cívic Cristalleries Planell
Carrer del Dr Ibáñez, 38

One of the façades on the corner of Carrer Anglesola and Carrer del Dr Ibáñez (Les Corts district) features a fantastic Modernist mosaic, reminding us of the industrial past of the building on which it is displayed.

This was the old Cristalleries Planell, a factory manufacturing artistic glassware – founded in 1913, it became one of the most important in Europe until it stopped operating in 1957. After lying derelict for years, the façade was restored in early 2017 and part of the old building was repurposed as an adult learning centre, a Catalan language school and a home for welfare institutions.

However, beyond its opulence and fame as a company, the old Cristalleries Planell conceals the history of the dreadful living conditions endured by its workers in the early 20th century. During that period, life for the people working in the glassworks sector was particularly hard. The rules allowed for 24-hour shifts and for children to be hired from the age of 9 onwards.

Children were particularly useful as their tender age meant they could be paid less while their smaller stature enabled them to move agilely in cramped spaces where grown-ups did not fit. Before the ovens could be lit, they needed to be cleaned and this task was reserved for children who, with no extra pay, had to start work an hour earlier than the rest of the staff.

In the light of these harsh conditions, in 1925, in the middle of General Primo de Rivera's dictatorship, the child workers of Cristalleries Planell led a strike which, organised by pickets, spread through the sector across the entire city. Faced with pressure from the striking children, industrial action finally ended when the employers agreed to pay for the hours spent cleaning and lighting the ovens. One of the main driving forces was an orphan child called Francesc Pedra, who was just 11 years old at the time.

In 2011, the City Council inaugurated a new street called Carrer de Francesc Pedra behind the factory's main façade. It was dedicated to that child who, as an old man, had died 11 years earlier.

JARDÍN DE JAUME VIÇENS I VIVES ⑬

Zoological sculpture garden

Avinguda Diagonal, 629
Metro María Cristina

Jardín Jaume Viçens i Vives must be the most unusual and least-known park in Barcelona. Right inside the entrance, visitors are confronted by a terrifying metal sculpture of a reindeer being devoured by wolves.

Venturing further into the gardens, other figures of animals emerge, including a family of boars walking in single file, a rather disconcerted-looking deer, and a headless gazelle.

Hardly anyone visits this park to contemplate the beauty of the sculptures, which almost seem to have wandered in by chance. They are made from a variety of materials – marble, plaster, bronze – without any common style or scale.

Over time, some of the animals have lost various bits and pieces and thus been turned into mutants or hybrids, quite moving to see. This little park hidden in a built-up area is just next to La Caixa savings bank.

ETERNAL LAMP IN PEDRALBES MONASTERY

(14)

The eternal lamp and St Joseph's fly

Baixada del Monestir, 9
93 256 3434
FGC: Reina Elisenda
Metro María Cristina, Palau Reial

The monastery of Pedralbes is a beautiful Gothic building founded in 1327 by Queen Elisenda de Montcada. It was inhabited by a community of Clarist nuns (the female branch of the Order of St Francis) until 1983. Currently, both the church and its pretty three-storey cloisters are open to the public, along with some of the rooms. In addition, one of the halls houses an interesting collection of medieval art.

In the chapterhouse, just next to the entrance to the monastery, there is a lamp most visitors would not even notice, but which has one peculiar feature: it never goes out.

To discover the story behind this little lamp we need to go back more than a hundred years: in July 1909, after the decision to send soldiers to fight in Morocco to keep control of Ceuta and Melilla, various left-wing groups rose up against the government. There were violent confrontations in which numerous churches and convents were burnt down in a series of events known as Tragic Week, which was particularly harsh in Barcelona.

Fearing for their lives, the Clarist nuns abandoned the monastery for a few days, but before they left they lit an oil lamp so that the Virgin would protect them and the building. When they returned, safe and sound, the monastery had not been attacked and the lamp was still burning. It is now kept permanently alight in remembrance of these events.

SAINT JOSEPH'S FLY

15

The proof of a painter's skill?

Monestir de Pedralbes
Baixada del Monestir, 9
Tel: 932 56 3434
Metro Reina Elisenda

In a large rectangular room that served as the nuns' dormitory on the second floor of Pedralbes monastery, the exhibition *Els Tresors del Monestir* (The Treasures of the Monastery) offers a selection of works of art, furniture and liturgical items amassed by the religious community over the centuries.

At the back of the room is an anonymous painting of the Holy Family which features a little-known oddity: a fly on Joseph's forehead.

If for some the fly, as a nuisance you swat away and yet always comes back to bother you, symbolizes Saint Joseph's suspicions about the infidelity of his wife after the Archangel Gabriel's annunciation, the most widely accepted theory is that, by looking like a real fly that has landed on the painting, the depicted insect is proof of the artist's skill.

Even Pliny the Elder (1st century AD) recorded the way the painter Apelles won a competition against his contemporary Parrassius. The first of them made a perfect copy of a still life featuring fruit to which he added a fly that seemed so real Parrassius felt the urge to swat it away, thereby having to admit the superiority of his rival.

In his *Lives of the Artists*, Giorgio Vasari tells an anecdote about Giotto: 'While Giotto was still young, he once painted on the nose of one of the portraits his master Cimabue was executing a fly that was so lifelike that when Cimabue returned to carry on with his work he tried several times to brush it off with his hand until he realized his mistake.'

However art critic Daniel Arasse thought that Giotto never painted the fly because this was not normal practice at that time. The fly, as a detail and symbol of the ability of the painter to fool the observer, as a sign of his talent and virtuoso skill, was an extremely common decorative motif from the mid-15th century to the early 16th century.

Other examples of paintings with flies on them include: *Allegory of the Arts* by Simon Luttichuys (1646); *Christ Supported by Two Angels* by Giovanni Santi (1480); *Saint Catherine of Alexandria* by Carlo Crivelli (c. 1491–94); *Madonna and Child* also by Crivelli (c. 1480); *Portrait of a Carthusian* by Petrus Christus (1446), and *Hurdy-Gurdy Player with a Fly* by Georges de la Tour (1631–36).

TIBIDABO
PLAÇA DEL TIBIDABO
Observatorio Fabra
Funicular del Tibidabo
Camí de l'Observatori
Carretera de Sant Cugat
Vall d'Hebron
Avinguda del Jordà
Ronda del Dalt
Penitents
PLAÇA DE ALFONSO COMÍN
Vallcarca
Parc Güell
Lesseps
PLAÇA DE LESSEPS
Travessera del Dalt
Fontana
GRÀCIA
Joanic
Diagonal
PLAÇA DE JOAN CARLES I
ESQUERRA DE L'EIXAMPLE
Verdaguer
PLAÇA DE FRANCESC MACIÀ
PL. DE SANT GREGORI TAUMATURG
PL. DE CASTELLÓ
PL. D'ADRIÀ
PL. DE JOAQUIM FOLGUERA
PLAÇA DE MOLINA
PLAÇA DE ROVIRA
PL. N. OLLER
Rambla del Prat
Passeig de la Bonanova
Via Augusta
Avinguda Diagonal
Passeig de Gràcia
Passeig de Sant Joan
0 200 400 600 800 1 000 m
1
2
3
4
5
6
7
8
9
10
11

North

L'EMPORDÀ. ODA NOVA A BARCELONA ①

An 'indecent, lesbian' sculpture

Jardins de Salvador Espriu
Metro Diagonal

In December 1961, to mark the centenary of the birth of Catalan poet Joan Maragall, the mayor José María de Porcioles unveiled the sculpture *L'Empordà. Oda nova a Barcelona* (New Ode to Barcelona Empordà) in Jardins de Salvador Espriu.

This work by the poet's son, sculptor Ernest Maragall (1903–91), shows two recumbent women, one naked and the other finely draped. Some people were quick to denounce the siting of this lesbian image in such a busy place, where passers-by might be shocked.

Maragall had to accept this and see his work exiled to a lonely corner of the distant Cervantes Park. In 1985, when democracy and peace had been restored, his nephew the mayor Pasqual Maragall returned the work to its original site.

It is worth taking a walk to Jardinets de Gràcia to contemplate these two women of Carrara marble from all angles, finding nothing remarkable about them other than their classical beauty.

Other 'irreverent' sculptures

The Font del Geni Català (Fountain of Catalan Genius, 1856) in Plaça del Palau, the work of Francesc Daniel Molina, consists of four lion's heads (representing the Llobregat, Ter, Ebro and Segre rivers), four seated statues (the Catalan provinces) and, above, a naked angel holding a star. A few days after the fountain was installed, the angel's genitals were mutilated with a hammer and hidden with a stone drape at the request of the bishop, who considered it scandalous that ladies should be regularly passing by to admire the statue. Although the drape was removed in the 1980s, the statue remains castrated.

In Ciutadella Park, near the Parliament building, the 1936 monument dedicated to the Catalan volunteers who fought alongside the French in the First World War is by Josep Clarà. It features a naked man with arms raised, holding a laurel branch and a sword, symbols of the struggle for freedom. Naked, but not completely: during the years of the Franco regime, his crotch was hidden by a vine leaf.

CLÍNICA BARRAQUER

2

For your eyes only

Muntaner, 314
93 209 5311
barraquer.com
Metro Muntaner

The clinic of Ignacio Barraquer, a renowned ophthalmologist, but also an architect and inventor with a deep passion for design, is unique in the fascinating details it brings out.

Barraquer founded his masterpiece in 1941: an Art Deco building with a metallic structure and rounded forms.

In the foyer, an Egyptian *udjat* (Eye of Horus) protects against the 'evil eye' and welcomes patients and visitors, who, if they raise their heads, can check the time from a clock unexpectedly fixed on the ceiling.

The waiting room is round and heavy with symbolism: walls are covered with the signs of the zodiac, Renaissance statues (some of which are decapitated human figures), comfortable leather sofas, custom-made doors and fittings, and mirrors positioned so that their reflections multiply endlessly, creating an optical illusion. (Some of these curious details can be seen on the website.)

Although the Barraquer clinic is visually astounding, paradoxically many of the patients are blind.

It focuses on the investigation, prevention, diagnosis, treatment, and control of all aspects of ocular health.

Although many patients will not be aware of the clinic's visual design details, they cannot fail to enjoy its practicality.

With the comfort of patients in mind, in designing his clinic Doctor Barraquer opted for curved walls, eliminating sharp angles.

He also chose soft lighting, which will not irritate the eyes of patients who have just undergone surgery or recovered their sight for the first time.

A GRENADE IN THE STREET 

The first battles of the anarchist and utopian socialists

Carrer Granada del Penedès, 12

An iron ball can be spotted on the outside of the wall surrounding No. 12 Carrer de la Granada del Penedès. You may wonder if this sphere, decorated with an iron star on top, is a grenade, a bomb, or simply a metallic ball.

Most people believe it to be a grenade dating from the battles of the anarchist and utopian socialists in the mid-19th century. This street used to be called just Granada (Grenade) street, but Penedès was added to avoid confusion with another street of the same name in Poblenou. Fixed to the wall with a metre-long iron structure, the grenade has become a neighbourhood symbol.

REFUGI 232

④

Fear of bombing during the Civil War

Plaça del Diamant, 10
932 196 134
Opens Sundays at 11am
Metro Fontana

More than 1,400 air-raid shelters were dug under the streets of Barcelona to protect the city's population during the bombing of the Spanish Civil War (underground train tunnels and the basements of some churches were also used). Although few such shelters have

survived, it's possible to visit some of them today, such as Refugi 307 (Shelter 307) in Poble Sec (see p. 170) or this one in Plaça del Diamant, also known as Refugi 232.

As with many other shelters, Refugi 232 was built thanks to a neighbourhood residents' committee and to the work of the entire local populace. It was the committee that provided the necessary funds and commissioned the planning works, which were carried out by volunteers.

Work got underway in 1937 and came to a halt at the end of 1938: the result was a network of brick-lined tunnels some 12 metres underground. The Plaça del Diamant shelter could hold around 300 people and had two access points, one on each side of the square, with different stairways to organise and direct the flow of residents towards the galleries where they could wait out the bombing raids.

Rows of stone benches were fitted on both sides of the shelter wall, with 40-cm seats marked out with lines … enough to sit down on and wait for the bombing to finish.

Oil or kerosene lamps hung from the walls; the smoke was let out thanks to two ventilation shafts, the only contact with the outside world. The shelter was also fitted with an electrical connection and had a couple of lightbulbs, although this was not used in case the power sub-station was affected by the bombing, leaving no possible way of using the electricity.

To avoid incidents, the shelter had its own rules of cohabitation. You could not take weapons or food down with you and it was forbidden to talk about politics or religion. There was no running water, though the shelter was fitted with toilets and had a small infirmary equipped with camp beds and a first-aid kit.

After the fall of Barcelona in January 1939, Franco's government kept the shelter intact due to the uncertainty surrounding the Second World War. Once it became clear that the shelter no longer served any purpose, the ventilation shafts were sealed off and it was left to its fate. Thanks to that, and to the humidity and temperature, the Plaça del Diamant shelter has remained intact to the present day.

It was reopened in 1999 and, after some of the square's oldest residents had been allowed to visit it, it was reconditioned so that guided tours could be organised from 2006.

THE FOUR FACES OF THE BOSQUE CINEMA

⑤

Stony expressions

Rambla del Prat, 16
Metro Fontana

The stone faces on the walls of the Bosque cinema, depicting the artists Pablo Picasso and Isidre Nonell, the doctor Jacinto Reventós, and the sculptor Pau Gargallo, have a curious story to tell.

The site where the cinema now stands used to be part of the La Fontana estate, property of Joaquim de Prat i de Roca, which included private woodland.

During the second half of the 19th century, a great many theatrical and concert performances were given in this park until finally, in 1905, a theatre was built and named the Gran Teatre del Bosc.

Pau Gargallo was commissioned to carry out the four sculptures that embellish the front of the building. In 1998, after many renovations, it began to be used as a cinema.

The stone faces were also modified but they were retained as part of the conversion.

A MASTERPIECE OF DESIGN

Barcelona's Clockwork Orange

Vía Augusta, 128
Metro Lesseps

The lobby of No. 128 Vía Augusta is well worth a visit. This office and residential block, designed by Antoni de Moragas in the 1970s, combines wood, concrete and vividly coloured ceramic tiles. Its extravagant entrance could well have been the setting for Kubrick's *Clockwork Orange* or one of the retro lounge bars that are currently back in vogue.

Antoni de Moragas (1913–1985), an extremely innovative architect and industrial designer, headed Catalonia's post-war architectural movement and was dean of the Colegio Oficial de Arquitectos de Catalunya y Baleares, the profession's governing body. His work focused on Barcelona's urban development programme and he designed many residential blocks, private homes, and the community centre on Carrer de Gomis. He also supervised the renovation of the Fémina cinema.

VALLVIDRERA RESERVOIR AND GROTT MINE

⑦

A city reservoir

Baixador de Vallvidrera railway station (FGC)

Although many residents aren't aware of it, the city has its own reservoir: the Pantano de Vallvidrera, which can easily be reached from Baixador de Vallvidrera train station, formerly known as Lake Valley.

This infrastructure was opened in 1850 to collect the abundant waters that came down from the Sierra Collserola mountains to supply the city. It's still pleasant to stroll around the area today. To channel the water, a narrow 1,400-metre-long tunnel was built, piercing the very heart of the mountain and coming out the other side of the sierra. The tunnel entrance can still be seen near the dam wall.

In the early 20th century, the Vallvidrera area started to become popular both as a nature spot and as a fashionable destination, attracting

the bourgeoisie who wanted to get out into the mountains, far from the hubbub of the industrial city.

Taking advantage of this, and the challenges facing transport links in the hilly area, the entrepreneur Carles Emili Montañés came up with the great idea of making use of the tunnel to install a little electric train to carry urban tourists. At the time, this was a technologically revolutionary idea and it proved a huge success. The tunnel was lit with 80 lightbulbs in different colours and the electric train ran along the line with its acetylene front light, carrying up to 36 passengers sat in rows of two.

We can still see the building that served as the station/café, and until recently the visitor centre (now closed). Lake Valley became a benchmark destination and the electric train worked to full capacity during the short two years it was in service.

The first signs of jealousy among members of the railway company did not take long to emerge, however. They claimed the infrastructure did not meet current rail regulations while the recently created Tibidabo amusement park argued that Lake Valley was also an amusement and therefore guilty of unfair competition.

Enemies of the successful station also had the support of Barcelona's civil governor, Ángel Osorio, and they finally got it closed down, with the reservoir area then falling into oblivion …

The tunnel's lower exit

The tunnel, known as the Grott Mine, still exists today; in fact, it can be seen through the bars of the upper exit near the former Lake Valley. So is there a lower exit? Well, yes, and it really is a complete secret. If you get off the train at Peu del Funicular station and walk round Monserrat College, you can see the stairway following the route of the funicular, just on the left of it. If you start climbing up, you can see that between the scrub and bushes an old structure with brick columns still exists. That is the tunnel's lower entrance. Apparently, several years ago someone built an improvised home there and they've closed it off with chains.

Oddly enough, there are also stairs on the right-hand side. If you go up to the top, you come to a street with a very strange name, the 'Carrer de ja hi som', which in Catalan translates as something like 'Now We're There Street'. It was baptised as such because that's the phrase that was always uttered by panting city locals who had walked up to save the price of a funicular ticket.

LOBBY OF BARCELONA'S XANASCAT YOUTH HOSTEL

⑧

Arab arches hidden in a youth hostel

Alberg Barcelona Xanascat Mare de Déu de Montserrat
Passeig de la Mare de Déu del Coll, 41-51
932 105 151
xanascat.gencat.cat/ca/albergs/albergs/barcelona-xanascat
alberg.barcelona@gencat.cat
Metro Vallcarca

The neoclassical exterior and Modernist touches of the building that today houses the Barcelona Xanascat youth hostel do little to suggest the arabesque exuberance of its lobby. With its colourful rows of arches inspired by Granada's Alhambra, it invites visitors on an imaginary journey through time to the period of Arab rule.

Designed in the early 20th century by the architect Juli Marial i Tey, the building was intended to be a summer house for the powerful Marsans family, and the residence of Josepa Marsans i Peix. However, the tumultuous history of the times meant that it became a direct witness of some of the period's greatest upheavals.

During the Civil War it housed a blood hospital run by the Republican Generalitat, subsequently becoming a barracks for the Moroccan troops of Franco's army. Once the Franco regime had taken over, it came under the administration of the Spanish Falange's Social Care unit.

During the Second World War, the building served as the headquarters of the Polish Public School, where war orphans boarded, returning once again to the Falange's Social Care unit when the war ended.

Señora Marsans spent hardly any time in her mansion. Although Casa Marsans is not particularly well known, the popular travel agency Viajes Marsans certainly is. Founded and run by Señora Marsans, it was the first of its kind in Spain.

Among those neo-Arabic archways inspired by the Patio of the Lions in Granada's Alhambra, we now find young tourists strolling alongside pupils from the Learning School run by the Generalitat's Department of Education. These students come from schools across Catalonia to spend a few days in the city finding out about its history and undertaking various educational activities.

MUSEUM OF ANTIQUE AUTOMATS ⑨

Historic attractions

Plaça del Tibidabo, 3-4
93 211 7942 – tibidabo.cat/ca/en-el-parc/atraccions/museu-dautomats
Weekends
Bus to Tibidabo departs from Plaça Cataluña

At the touch of a button, you can activate a miniature ski station, a guitarist, a mandolin-playing clown, or a roller coaster. These are just a few of the most extraordinary devices at Tibidabo's Automat Museum.

They are all collectors' items in perfect condition and date from the late 19th century. Most of them, such as the tightrope walkers, the guillotine (which demonstrates the precise moment of decapitation), and the mechanics' workshop, are veritable relics of a bygone age.

To visit the museum you need to pay the park's general admission fee, but this is no ordinary amusement park, as most attractions date from the 1970s and have a very different feeling and style to their modern counterparts.

Located at the top of Tibidabo mountain, at an altitude of 512 metres (the highest point of the Collserola range), its strange name stems from the Latin *tibi dabo* ('I will give you'), the words spoken by the Devil in his splendid vanity when he tried to tempt Jesus as they looked down on all the kingdoms of the world. Tibidabo does in fact offer the most spectacular views – particularly on a clear day when the wind has blown away the grey-brown cloud of pollution floating over the city.

When visiting the Tibidabo amusement park, it is also worth checking out the Marionetarium, which gives inventive performances using vintage puppets.

NEARBY

Foster's scenic viewpoint ⑩

Carretera de Vallvidrera al Tibidabo s/n
Reservations and information: 934 069 354

Most people will be familiar with Norman Foster's Torre de Collserola, famous from Barcelona's 1992 Olympic Games, but few know that it is possible to gain access to its highest point and enjoy fantastic views of the city, weather permitting. The 288-metre tower is at the top of a natural peak already 445 metres above sea level, which add up to a truly spectacular vantage point. A panoramic elevator travels 135 metres in 2½ minutes to reach the top.

GATEWAY TO THE MIRALLES RESIDENCE

An authentic and unknown work by Gaudí

Carrer de Manuel Girona, 55–57 – Metro María Cristina

Surrounded by modern buildings in the Sarrià district, an impressive arched entrance in genuinely Gaudí-like style seems to stick out like an architectural sore thumb.

And no, it isn't a Gaudí reproduction or a piece inspired by the master architect and installed in the middle of nowhere, but an actual authentic work by him. So what's it doing here?

At one time, the imposing gateway was the entrance to the residence of Hermenegild Miralles, the owner of a company making construction equipment. Miralles was a good friend of Eusebi Güell, the prolific and original architect's main patron, and a close collaboration developed between Miralles and Gaudí. The industrial facilities were used for some of the tests and experiments with materials that Gaudí carried out for far more well-known and popular works than this one.

Miralles originally commissioned Gaudí to design the entire building, but in the end the project went to Domènec Sugranyes, another of the architect's collaborators.

But what did get a quintessentially Gaudí seal was the gateway, which still stands today, along with the perimeter fence of which some sections have survived.

The lobed archway has one entrance for carriages and another for pedestrians, perhaps drawing on old Roman city gateways. A metallic structure like a fishing net is stretched over an awning made of fibre cement imitating the shell of a tortoise.

At the top of the archway you can see a three-dimensional cross, very much a symbol of Gaudí's architecture, which could be inspired by cypress tree cones once they have dried and opened up.

During renovation works in 2000, a life-size bronze statue of Antoni Gaudí was erected, the work of sculptor Joan Camps.

The old Miralles residence disappeared, and was replaced by modern buildings in the 1970s. Even so, the streets inside the complex to which Gaudí's gateway still serves as an entry point are wide, sunny and pedestrianized, with gardens including facilities aimed at children. Without doubt a great outing to enjoy Modernism far from the hubbub involved in visiting the rest of the master's infinitely more popular and better-known architectural works.

N
Can Masdeus
Camí de Sant Llàtzer
1
Ronda del Dalt
Mundet
C. d'Horta Cerdanyola
Valldaura
PLAÇA DE KARL MARX
Canyelles
Carrer de les Torres
Trinitat Nova
Ronda del Dalt
C. J. Manrique
2
3
PLAÇA DE BOTTICELLI
HORTA
4
C. de Salses
Carrer del Canigó
Passeig de Fabra i Puig
Passeig
Via Júlia
Via Júlia
Carrer de Porto
C. de Dante Alighieri
C. de Crehuet
Horta
Parc del Turó de la Peira
6
Passeig d'Urrutia
7
P. de Verdum
Llucmajor
Carrer d'Argullós
Meridiana
Avinguda de Rio de Janeiro
Valldaura
C. de Valldemossa
Torras i Bages
5
Passeig
Av. de l'Estatut de Catalunya
C. de Llobregós
C. de Llobregós
Vilapicina
8
10
C. de Palomar
C. de Grau
Carrer de Agustí i Milà
Sant Andreu
P. de Torras i Bages
C. de Malats
Virrei Amat
PLAÇA DE VIRREI AMAT
C. del Dr. Pi i Molist
Carrer de Pedrell
Carrer de Maragall
C. d'Amilcar
Cartellà
C. d'Arnau d'Oms
Fabra i Puig
C. de la Reira d'Horta
Avinguda
Gran de Sant Andreu
Sant Andreu
C. de Sòcrates
P. de Fabra i Puig
9
Fabra i Puig
C. de la Gran Vista
11
Parc del Guinardó
EL GUINARDÓ
Maragall
Av. de la Mare de Déu de Montserrat
Carrer de Varsòvia
R. de la Muntanya
12
Congrès
Carrer de Concepción Arenal
Carrer de Serge
PL. DE LA FONT CASTELLANA
Alfons X
Ronda del Guinardó
Guinardó
Carrer de Garcilaso
de la Sagrera
Sant Martí
Rambla
Camp de l'Arpa
Passeig Maria Claret
Sant Antoni
Carrer de Felip II
Meridiana
Travessera de Gràcia
Indústria
Carrer del Freser
C. de Coll i Vehí
C. de Besalú
Carrer de las Navas de Tolosa
Navas
Avinguda de Gaudí
Carrer de Llepant
Còrsega
Rosselló
Provença
Mallorca
13
Ronda
Carrer de Menorca
Huelva
Guipúscoa
Clot
C. de Mallorca
València
Sant Martí
La Pau
Sagrada Família
Encants
Carrer de Cartagena
Dos de Maig
Carrer de la Independència
Carrer d'Aragó
Bac de Roda
14
Sagrada Família
Avinguda
SANT MARTÍ
Catalanes
Corts
Besòs
EIXAMPLE
Avinguda Diagonal
PLAÇA DE LES GLÒRIES CATALANES
Parc de Clot
Gran Via de les Corts Catalanes
Carrer Perú
Carrer Pere IV
Monumental
Passatge del Marquès de Santa Isabel
15
Gran Via de les Corts Catalanes
Glòries
Carrer de Ribes
Meridiana
Bolívia
Avinguda
Tànger
Passatge del Taulat
27
Besòs Mar
16
26
Carrer de Josep Pla
Pallars
Sancho de Àvila
Pere IV
Carrer de Bac de Roda
Rambla
Diagonal
Prim
17
18
Carrer dels Almogàvers
Pallars
25
Pujades
El Maresme Fòrum
Marina
VILA OLÍMPICA
Llacuna
Poblenou
Selva de Mar
Llull
Selva del Mar
Parc de Diagonal Mar
Avinguda
Bogatell
Badajoz
Rambla del Poblenou
Bilbao
Roda
C. dels Pellaires
Taulat
Parlament de Catalunya
Carrer de Ramon Trias Fargas
Marina
Ramon Turró
Doctor Trueta
d'Àvila
23
Passeig del Taulat
24
Cementerio del Poblenou
Ronda del Litoral
Parque Carlos I
22
21
d'Icària
C. de Carmen Amaya
Parc del Poblenou
19
Avinguda
Salvador Espriu
20
Carrer de
Ciutadella Vila Olímpica
Playa de la Nova Mar Bella
Playa de la Mar Bella
Playa del Bogatell
0
500
1 000 m

East

POEMA VISUAL SCULPTURAL GROUP

1

The circle of life with its ups and downs

Jardins de Marià Cañardo Lacasta
Passeig dels Castanyers, 14
Daily 10am–8.30pm
Metro Mundet
Bus 27, 60, 76 and H4

This artistic ensemble entitled *Poema visual* (Visual Poem) – the work of the sculptor Joan Brossa – was unveiled in 1984 to mark the opening of the World Cycling Championships in the Horta Velodrome. It stands in the adjoining gardens named after the cyclist Marià Cañardo Lacasta.

In what he called 'visual poems', Brossa combined his two great passions, poetry and art, in one single concept. This visual poem features a range of sculptural elements arranged along the uphill slope of the hill where the velodrome was built. The first thing you see is a capital letter 'A' made of artificial stone, standing 16 metres tall and acting as the entrance to a green space full of carob, olive and cypress trees.

A range of punctuation marks are scattered across the lawn: a full stop, a comma, three dots, a question and an exclamation mark, brackets, a colon, inverted commas, a dash and square brackets.

Towards the top of the enclosure, looking across the velodrome, there is another capital 'A', though this one is broken, its base resting on the ground and with lots of broken bits lying around.

The ensemble represents the circle of life, from the whole 'A' through to the broken one, from life to death, where the initial capital 'A' symbolises birth while the final broken one stands for death and destruction.

The varying punctuation marks arranged between the two refer to the ups and downs we go through in life, what the artist called a 'path with pauses and intonations'. What we have here is a reflection on life and death through a series of objects symbolising notions based on images. 'The life of living beings is subject to a downwards evolution that ends in destruction,' the artist explains.

© Canaan

Joan Brossa (1919–1989) was a multifaceted artist who wrote poetry in Catalan. He was linked to magical surrealism and abstract Informalism. His work moves between complementary fields, including poetry, theatre, painting, signage, film, magic, musical activities and translations of Rimbaud. Other works by Brossa in Barcelona include: *Llagost* (Colegio de Aparejadores); *Lletres gimnastes* (Passeig de Sant Joan); *El antifaz* (La Rambla, between Carrer Portaferrisa and Carrer del Carme); *Barcino* (Plaça de la Catedral) and *Monumento al libro* (Gran Vía, next to Passeig de Gràcia).

PAVELLÓ DE LA REPÚBLICA

2

Replica of the space for which Picasso painted Guernica

Avinguda Cardenal Vidal i Barraquer, 34-26
crai.ub.edu/ca/coneix-el-crai-biblioteques/biblioteca-pavello-republica
Metro Montbau

It is not generally known that Picasso's celebrated *Guernica* was painted for the Paris International Exposition of 1937.

During the Civil War, the Spanish Republic participated in the Expo with a pavilion designed by rationalist architects Josep Lluís Sert and Luis Lacasa, whose Modernist vision pulled in the visitors.

The Pavilion of the Republic, at the Trocadero gardens in Paris, displayed *Guernica* along with other works such as Joan Miró's *El Segador* (The Reaper) and *Fuente de Mercurio* (Mercury Fountain), a mobile by Alexander Calder in tribute to the Almadén miners that can be seen today at Barcelona's Miró Foundation. The sculptures included *La Montserrat* by Julio González and *El pueblo español tiene un camino que conduce a una estrella* (The Spanish People Have a Path that Leads to a Star) by Alberto Sánchez, symbols of the struggle for freedom. These works by leading artists became testimonials to the tragic situation of the Spanish people, as well as a cry for help addressed to international public opinion.

A replica of this pavilion, the Pavelló de la República, was built for the 1992 Olympic Games near Ronda de Dalt in Horta district. The simple and functional three-storey building, shaped like a storage container, houses one of the world's largest libraries on the Second Republic, the Civil War, exile, Francoism and the transition to democracy. In the open space of the central courtyard is a reproduction of *Guernica* as exhibited in its original location.

NEARBY
Mistos *sculpture* ③

In front of the pavilion stands an original sculpture, *Mistos*, a monumental book of matches by Claes Oldenburg and his wife Coosje van Bruggen. It was erected in 1992 as part of an ambitious municipal programme to endow the entire city, even the suburbs, with sculptures by well-known artists. *Mistos* is eye-catching because of its height (21 metres), but especially because it is an immediately recognizable everyday object. So it often eclipses *Guernica*, the real jewel of Vidal i Barraquer avenue.

HORTA VELLA FARM

④

A hidden garden

Granja Vella d'Horta
Avinguda Cardenal Vidal i Barraquer, 15
93 429 1803
marti-codolar.net
Open during daytime on demand
Metro Montbau

In the mid-19th century, wealthy businessman Lluís Martí i Codolar (1843–1915) bought a large property in Horta Vella la Granja as his leisure park. He soon had part of the land laid out as gardens and cultivated the rest so successfully that he was awarded the Grand Cross of the Order of Merit for Agriculture.

He was also passionately keen on building up an exotic animal collection, for which he acquired various species: ostriches, flamingos, pelicans, swans, kangaroos, llamas, camels and even an Indian elephant.

In 1891, in deep financial trouble, Martí was forced to sell his collection of animals to the local authorities, thus founding Barcelona Zoo which opened on the annual festival of Our Lady of Mercy (La Mercè) in 1892. In 1946, his heirs sold the property to the religious order the Salesians of Don Bosco.

The 19th-century mansion is now a Salesian seminary, but you can ask to visit the gardens. A short walk in such a beautiful place soon reveals the reason for its success. In the past it attracted such illustrious visitors as Ferdinand VII, Alfonso XIII and Don Bosco, founder of the Salesian Order, while poets and painters, including Eduardo Marquina and Santiago Rusiñol, found inspiration for some of their work there.

The gardens are filled with a variety of plants, ancient trees, jets and fountains whose lapping water is an invitation to relax. Beautiful sculptures, such as those representing the different ages of man or the labours of Hercules, the mythical founder of Barcelona, are dotted here and there. Cigarral de la Santa, a peaceful area created in the early 20th century in honour of Saint Teresa, deserves special mention.

THE HORTA WASHERWOMEN ⑤

Old-style laundry

Aiguafreda, 10-30
Metro Horta

Strolling around Aiguafreda, one of the most typical streets in Horta-Guinardó, it is difficult to imagine that, 100 years ago, the little gardens here formed part of the biggest laundry in Barcelona.

Several metres beneath the streets of Horta-Guinardó, water ran directly from mountain streams. It was so clear and clean that it could be drunk straight from the wells that were part of each Aiguafreda house.

Over three centuries, until the Civil War, the washerwomen did their laundry first with very cold water then with hot water.

The difference in temperature, together with the purity of the water and the women's efficiency, gave the clothes an unequalled freshness and cleanliness when they were sent back to Barcelona.

One of the paradoxes of the city between the 16th and 19th centuries was that the supply of water bore little relation to citizens' needs. Wealthy people often had no water for laundry purposes, nor did they have enough space to lay their washing out to dry.

The water also used to contain a high level of chalk, damaging the smart clothing made by famous designers of the times, much of it imported from Paris.

All this contributed to the development of the Horta laundry service, which employed a great many people.

Every Monday, errand boys were responsible for collecting sacks of washing, piled up at a point between Vía Laeitana and Carrer del Consell de Cent, returning them on Fridays so that the bourgeoisie could dress up in all their finery during the weekend.

CAN PEGUERA NEIGHBOURHOOD

6

The only nucleus of 'cheap housing' that remains true to its original style

Carrer Vila-Seca
Metro Vilapiscina

Can Peguera is a peaceful neighbourhood of low-rise housing at the foot of Turó de la Peira district. In contrast to most areas across the city, here the locals know each other, greet each other and spend much of the day together outside their homes. It is one of the few Barcelona neighbourhoods that feels less like Barcelona and more like a remote hamlet.

One of the reasons behind this sociability is its humble urban planning, very much at street level, with a shared common history.

Can Peguera was once one of Barcelona's four 'cheap housing' nuclei, built after purchasing land from the Marquess of Castellvell, where she kept a rural estate bearing that name. For a time the neighbourhood was known as Grupo Ramon Albó.

The phenomenon of these working-class housing nuclei goes back to the 19th and early 20th centuries.

In 1911 a *casas baratas* (cheap housing) law was enacted, encouraging the construction of simple, single-storey working-class housing on the outskirts of urban hubs. They were normally built by public initiative or through cooperatives. These sorts of neighbourhoods spread throughout the nation, though the intense industrialization of the Basque Country and Catalonia meant they were particularly widespread in those regions.

When the news broke in Barcelona that an International Expo was going to be held in 1929, a process akin to what occurred in the run-up to the 1992 Olympics took place, with the relocation of people living in shanty towns made up of ramshackle housing, some of which were in Montjuïc where the Expo was due to be held.

These new nuclei of cheap housing were populated by former shanty towners and families who had emigrated from inland Catalonia or from the south of Spain, looking for work on Expo construction projects.

During the Spanish Civil War, the working-class profile of these neighbourhoods meant that many became anti-Fascist strongholds, especially Can Peguera, which was essentially under the rule of the anarchist syndicalists.

It was here that the CNT-FAI's two main magazines were published (*Solidaridad Obrera* and *Tierra y Libertad*). The church was taken over by the locals and turned into a 'house of the people'. During the Franco regime many of the residents suffered great hardships in the Civil Guard headquarters (now the neighbourhood school).

Other cheap housing nuclei were built during the dictatorship, although Can Peguera is the only one to remain true to its original style without undergoing destruction, neglect or fierce gentrification.

Other cheap housing nuclei in the city

- Grupo Eduard Aunós (near Passeig de la Zona Franca)
- Grupo Baró de Viver
- Grupo Milans del Bosch (now Can Peguera, under demolition, with one house turned into a museum)

PLAQUE COMMEMORATING THE GUERRILLA FACERÍAS

7

Anarchist and gentleman

Pla de les Mares de la Plaça de Mayo
Metro Lluchmajor

At the end of the Spanish Civil War, a few thousand former Republican fighters vowed to go underground and continue the fight against Franco. Hardened anarchists and communists were trained as commandos and used to sabotage factories, railways and power grids, to raid banks and jewellers, and to carry out assassination attempts on prominent members of the regime. The frequent arrests of activists led to many imprisonments as well as death sentences from the late 1940s onwards. This weakened the movement and it was dissolved in the late 1960s. In Catalonia, the most notorious guerrillas were Wenceslao Jiménez, Marcelino Massana, Quico Sabaté, Ramon Vila Capdevila (*Caracremada* or 'Burnt Face') and Josep Lluís i Facerías (alias *el Face*).

El Face (1920–57), also known as Petronio as well as *el Señorito*, 'the Young Gentleman', because of his elegant style, campaigned from the age of 16 with the anarchist union, the National Confederation of Labour (CNT). During the war, he volunteered to fight for the militia in Aragon. He was captured in 1939 and spent several years in prison. Once released, he threw himself back into the armed struggle and pulled off coups of rare audacity, such as the attack on the Pedralbes building (21 October 1951), a brothel on the road to Esplugues used by philandering members of high society. During this incident a well-known Barcelona businessman and Franco supporter, Antonio Massana Sanjuán, was killed in bed with his underage mistress (his niece, according to popular gossip).

On 30 August 1957, *el Face* went to a rendezvous with a gang member in the Sant Andreu district, not suspecting that the police were in the know and had laid an ambush for him. He was shot by gunmen hidden in the neighbouring buildings, with no chance of defending himself.

At the corner of Carrer del Doctor Pi i Molist in Plaça de las Madres de la Plaza de Mayo, a circular plaque next to the fountain marks the site where Facerías was shot, on 30 August 1957 at 10.45. An inscription alongside commemorates the victims of another military dictatorship, that of Argentina.

TOMB OF PERE VINTRÓ SAGRISTÀ ⑧

A hidden gem of Catalan Modernism

Cementerio de Sant Andreu
Carrer Garrofers, 35–47
cbsa.cat
Daily 8pm–6pm
Metro Lluchmajor, Fabra i Puig

Located in Section One of Sant Andreu cemetery, the tomb of the Barcelona landowner Pere Vintró Sagristà is a hidden gem of Catalan Modernism dating from 1902. Little known, this exceptional

work was executed by the architect Simó Cordomí.

The front part of the tomb features a spectacular figure from ancient Egypt, which appears to be keeping watch over the tomb, its arms open over a grille. The references to ancient Egypt are common in tombs due to the rich funerary culture of that civilisation. However, there are signs that in the original architecture this feature depicted a skull and scythe, common vanitas motifs. The tomb also boasts Christian iconography and inscriptions – the Cross at the back, the side with a message reading 'Death takes everything away. Only Christ gives light' and the Alpha and Omega symbols, along with the vegetal motifs (so characteristic of Modernism) in the stone relief and the grille over the opening to the hypogeum.

Pere Vintró Sagristà was a prominent Barcelona agrarian landowner, the scion of the agricultural dynasty started by Pere Vintró Vintró in the 18th century. His property included estates in the current districts of La Sagrera, El Clot, Camp de l'Arpa, el Guinardó (where he owned the famous Mas Vintró), Sant Martí and Sant Andreu, but it was in the latter two neighbourhoods that he constructed several residential buildings, even becoming mayor of Sant Andreu. Due to his links with that district, when Pere Vintró Sagristà died in 1902, his son Pere Vintró Mariné decided to lay him to rest there and thus, as was often the case for the city's bourgeoisie, he commissioned a pantheon from the Modernist architect Simó Cordomí.

Although Cordomí's most well-known works are in Camprodon and Granollers, where he was the municipal architect, his most prominent works in Barcelona are his two pantheons: that of Pere Vintró Sagristà and that of Dr Robert in Montjuïc cemetery.

There is a stone bench where visitors can watch over the deceased and contemplate this Modernist work.

THE CARRER DE SÒCRATES BOMB ⑨

Souvenir of a bombardment

Metro Sant Andreu

In the working-class district of Sant Andreu, which was a village on the outskirts of Barcelona until 1897, a bomb can be seen embedded in the façade of a Modernist building at the junction of Carrer Gran de Sant Andreu and Carrer de Sòcrates.

This missile dates from September 1843, when troops under the command of Colonel Joan Prim suppressed a popular insurrection against the conservative government in Madrid, known as the 'Jamància' because many of the volunteers enlisted only for the food (*jamar* is the Romany word for 'eat'). As a reward for his courage, Prim was promoted to general and later became president of the Spanish government (1869–1870).

Prim's artillery bombardment of Sant Andreu inflicted a great deal of damage, but not all of the missiles exploded. The owner of the building on this street corner has kept one of them as a trophy. During a restoration project in the early 20th century, the bomb was set into the wall to commemorate these events.

NEARBY

Gardens in Carrer de Grau ⑩

Between Carrer d'Agustí i Milá and Carrer Gran de Sant Andreu is a street that harks back to an earlier age with its low houses and gardens. At No. 41 you can see a curious collection of multicoloured ceramics, representing some of the sites in the neighbourhood and around Barcelona in a naive style.

TURÓ DE LA ROVIRA

11

Remains of the Horta anti-aircraft battery

Parc dels Tres Turons
Bus 24, 28, 86 and 119

Offering a superb 360° panorama, Horta's anti-aircraft battery is the best viewpoint in Barcelona. Paradoxically, it was in this marvellous setting that one of the worst episodes of the Civil War took place, the Republican troops having fought to the death here against their Nationalist foes. Their heroic resistance was even cited as an example by Winston Churchill in 1940, just before the Blitz: 'I do not at all underrate the severity of the ordeal which lies before us; but I believe our countrymen will show themselves capable of standing up to it, like the brave men of Barcelona.'

The air raids by Italian and German forces, supporting Franco's army by systematically bombing the civilian population, destroyed the city. In all, there were 385 raids that dropped 1,500 tons of bombs, resulting in 1,903 conflagrations that killed over 2,700 people.

In addition to Turó de la Rovira, the town has defences against air raids at Turó del Carmel, Sant Pere Mártir, Tibidabo, Montjuïc, Barceloneta, and Poblenou.

The weaponry consisted of a few anti-aircraft guns and a small fleet of planes, not enough to halt the great offensive. The guns used were mostly of English origin, Vickers 105s built in 1923.

The two types of fighter plane that were most successful in discouraging enemy attacks were the Polikarpov I-15 (nicknamed 'the seagull') and I-16 ('the fly'). Both of these Soviet aircraft were acrobatic and versatile, but their guns were not very powerful.

Today, the vestiges of the anti-aircraft battery at Turó de la Rovira and the air-raid shelter have deteriorated because of lack of maintenance and the fact that, until the early 21st century, the surrounding neighbourhood was a shanty town. The authorities have launched a project to safeguard this site of great historical interest, however.

KAGYU SAMYE DZONG

(12)

The main Buddhist centre in Spain

Rambla de la Muntanya, 97
93 436 2626
samye.es
Tuesday, Wednesday and Thursday 6.30pm-8pm
Metro Guinardó

The main Buddhist centre in Spain was founded in 1977 by his Holiness the 16th Karmapa. It preserves and spreads the teachings of Buddha and is dedicated to the promotion of the physical, mental, and spiritual well-being of its adherents.

The centre belongs to the Tibetan order of Buddhism, Karma Kagyu, and its official name is Karma Lodrö Gyamtso Ling, which means 'place of illuminated activity where an ocean of intelligence exists.'

The spacious sanctuary has a little shop selling books, incense, figurines, clothes, and various objects associated with meditation and Buddhism.

From time to time, the centre is visited by Tibetan lamas who come to lead seminars on philosophy and Buddhist meditation.

In addition, they offer a variety of courses; for example, on the history of Buddhism in India, or reflections on the seven points of mental stimulation.

Other activities include film shows, yoga classes, courses on different therapies, and the organization of spiritual retreats in the mountains around Barcelona.

In farms far from the city, various types of retreats take place, intended for beginners as well as long-term practitioners. Those aspiring to become lamas undertake retreats lasting at least three years.

There are also weekend retreats, such as that at Ñung-Ne, which develop compassion, one of the five elements by which pupils learn to recognize the play of energy in body and mind; or the meditational retreat, Shiné, which cultivates internal calm.

Karma Kagyu

The Kagyu lineage is one of the four principal schools of Tibetan Buddhism, the three others being Nyingma, Sakya, and Gelug. The origins of the Kagyu school go back to the teachings of the Indian mystics Tilopa and Naropa, introduced to Tibet by the translator Marpa. Other grand masters of meditation, such as Milarepa, Gampopa, and Rechungpa, are also associated with this lineage.

The Kagyu method is based on the doctrine of Mahamudra (Great Seal) and on meditation. Currently the school has hundreds of centres around the world.

LA PRIMITIVA, BAR & ORNITHOLOGICAL SOCIETY

13

Beer among the birds

Avinguda Meridiana, 157
93 347 5520
Tuesday to Sunday, 9.30am-8pm
Metro Clot

La Primitiva bar and ornithological society opened its doors over 100 years ago and little has changed since. You only have to glance at the shabby walls, the calendars several decades out of date, and the rickety furniture to appreciate the dilapidated state of the place.

Don Antonio, a canary and finch enthusiast, decided to found an ornithological society that welcomed both birds and their owners to either chat or sing.

Over the years, La Primitiva has become a meeting place for the members of this exclusive club of bird fanciers, who come to the bar for an aperitif, a coffee, or a beer, and to play dominoes or cards. Their average age is 60, but this does not detract from the lively atmosphere that promises an original way of passing time.

Every Saturday, birdsong contests are organized on the patio behind the premises. To take part, you only need to pay €12 a year and to keep a canary.

One of the great benefits of belonging to the society is that members' birds can sleep in the bar, so the little creatures are less lonely and will learn to sing along with their friends ...

Even though the bar may seem to be exclusively for men, it is open to everyone.

UNIÓN DE CANARICULTORES DE BARCELONA

(14)

Karaoke for canaries

Avinguda Meridiana, 91
93 232 4204
canariosbarcelona.org
Tuesday and Friday 5pm–8pm
Metro Clot

The Barcelona canary-fanciers' union, set up seventy-five years ago, organizes an annual song competition for 1,200 canaries.

On the day of the contest, as the birds are more at ease singing in the dark, they are separated and their cages covered with a black cloth. This club of canary fanciers is also the ideal place to find advice on how to improve their song.

A canary imitates other sounds, so if it hears a CD playing first-class songs, its own performance will probably improve. Similarly, if a poor performer is placed next to a good one, the learner will soon make progress.

The annual competition has three classes: song, colour, and carriage. There are three different styles of birdsong to be judged: timbrado espagnol, roller, and malinois.

As for the colour and carriage contests, the most impressive thing about the show is that you can see for yourself the endless genetic variations between birds.

Some canaries have extravagant feathering and crests, while those entered in the colour class flaunt all the colours of the rainbow.

MONUMENT TO THE METRE

15

The role of Barcelona in the definition of the metre, in 1792

Arco del Meridiano – Plaça de les Glòries Catalanes
Metro Glòries and Monumental

Plaça de les Glòries Catalanes was chosen as the site of a monument commemorating the 200th anniversary of the measurement of the terrestrial meridian, which was used to determine the length of the metre. The inauguration ceremony took place before work on the surrounding site was completed, because time was running out for the

launch of the 1992 Olympic Games in Barcelona. The 40-metre steel monument, the work of François Scali and Alain Domingo and known as the Meridian Arc, represents the orographic profile (i.e. showing the terrain's relief), to scale, of the distance between Dunkirk and Barcelona. There is a reason for the length of 40 metres: under the new system, the Earth's total circumference as measured along the terrestrial meridians (or lines of longitude) running from North Pole to South Pole was defined as 40 million metres (or 40,000 kilometres). Beyond being a tribute to the metre as a system of measurement, the arc is dedicated to all the scientists involved in the definition of the metre using primitive instruments, in particular Jean-Baptiste Delambre and Pierre-François Méchain. On one side of the monument is an inscription describing their work.

The definition of the metre since 1791

Surprisingly enough, the word 'metre' has only been in existence for a little over two centuries. Before it came into being, there was no standard measurement for calculating distances: hands, feet, or other local units were used. In 1790, the French National Assembly proposed a universal measurement standard, based on natural phenomena and therefore acceptable to all nations. The chosen measurement was 1/10,000,000 of the quadrant of the Earth's circumference (from the North Pole through Paris to the Equator), to be known as the metre (from the Greek word *metron*, meaning 'measure'). Because it was impossible to measure the entire quarter of the meridian, the solution adopted was to measure part of it and calculate the total. The meridian arc chosen was that between Dunkirk and Barcelona. After several years of work, a platinum bar was made in 1799. This standard metre, today symbolic (although no longer accurate), is preserved at the Bureau International des Poids et Mesures (International Bureau of Weights and Measures) in Sèvres (France). In 1875, seventeen countries signed the Metre Convention. In 1889, the Conférence Générale des Poids et Mesures sanctioned a platinum/iridium alloy prototype of the metre that would not be subject to any variations in length. Since the 20th century, technology has allowed the metre to be defined with extreme precision but has also made it very difficult for the general public to understand.

For more information on Barcelona's role in the epic of defining the metre, see page 156.

OLD PROMOTIONAL ADVERTISING FOR 'ENVASES UNIVERSAL J. RIUS S.A.' ⑯

A cardboard box with a sad story

Carrer Badajoz, 150
Metro Glòries

Around No. 150 Carrer Badajoz, or looking towards the sea from the gardens alongside Agbar tower and adjoining the Museu del Disseny, is an old piece of promotional advertising.

This would appear to be an open cardboard box of colossal dimensions, and at first glance looks like a water tank, but when you see the hollow inside you realize that's not its function.

The box is not made from cardboard at all but from concrete, though it's finished right down to the last detail, giving an impression of the slightly undulating texture of cardboard. On the sides you can make out the words 'Envases Universal J.Rius S.A.' and a six-pointed star, the logo of said company.

At No. 175 Carrer d'Àvila there was for many years a cardboard container-manufacturing company called *Cartonería Española José Rius* which, operating under several different names, was at the forefront of the sector and patented a range of storage models.

In 1973 the company's rise was cut short by a devastating fire caused by one of the cutting machines overheating.

Due to the amount of flammable materials the fire spread quickly, resulting in the death of some of the employees who were trapped by the flames.

The families of those who did not come home were gripped with terror, and it took a long time to discover one of the bodies.

In the end it was Dan who found the human remains of the last missing worker, after suffering various injuries sniffing around the embers of the old factory. Dan was a dog belonging to a Barcelona local named Antonio Muñoz who generously offered to help in the rescue efforts.

Although the company had other facilities, the survivors of the fire at the Poblenou premises were laid off and ended up suing the company.

The cardboard/concrete box stands there to this day, marking the tragic event.

INSCRIPTION 'ES VICIO ES ALQUILER'

⑰

Solution to the mystery

Carrer Marina, 112
Metro Marina (L1)

At No. 112 Carrer Marina, at one end of the bridge is an old building featuring the enigmatic phrase: 'ES VICIO ES ALQUILER' (IT'S A VICE, IT'S RENTAL) in white letters on the wall.

Many locals pass by here on a regular basis, and a good number must have asked themselves what the words are doing there.

The answer lies in the origins of the building.

If you look closely at the façade, in addition to the text highlighted in white there are other letters making up the entire phrase, which reads 'GAY SILLAS MESAS SERVICIO PARA BANQUETES SECCION DE ALQUILER', meaning 'GAY CHAIRS TABLES SERVICE FOR BANQUETS RENTAL SECTION'.

Casa Gay was a furniture hire company with various outlets throughout the city. In the case of the premises at No. 112 Carrer Marina, the land registry records that it belonged to a Señora Gay, and that when she died childless part of her legacy went to a niece who apparently gave the property over for use by the religious Order of the Mercedarians.

After using the building for charitable works, the Order let the building fall into disuse for some years, and finally it was occupied by a group of squatters who, among other things, organized artistic workshops.

According to one member of a group that spent time there, when they saw they could reach the original slogan from the windows they came up with an idea.

They simply changed the colour of some of the letters on the wall to alter the commercial meaning of the original message.

And so the famous phrase 'IT'S A VICE, IT'S RENTAL' was born. A message that is both enigmatic and clear-cut, and which passers-by have been wondering about for years.

The building has been included in plans for a future urban green area, which may lead to an extension of the adjacent-existing park.

MUSEU DE CARROSSES FÚNEBRES

18

Transport to the afterlife

Carrer de la Mare de Déu de Port, 56–58
Saturday and Sunday 10am–2pm
Bus 21, 107

The Hearse Museum is not recommended for sensitive souls. Located in the basement of a branch of the municipal funerary services, it has a collection of various types of carriage and funeral cars from the 19th and 20th centuries.

This is a strange, damp, and rather improbable place. It displays all kinds of conveyances for the deceased, from those decked out in white for children and adolescents to Gothic carriages in the so-called 'French' style. Most come complete with mannequins elegantly dressed for the occasion, some in white and others in black. The same applies to the horses, featuring an array of funerary ornaments typical of their day.

Although the set pieces are very well done, it is a pity that the space is so restricted. Nevertheless, there are about twenty vehicles, some drawn by model horses, and showcases displaying the outfits of employees and horses in funerary procession.

This lugubrious, even melodramatic, atmosphere is heightened by the presence of an immense carriage entirely lined in black cloth. This was intended for widows who could afford to pay for lavish funerals, which were mainly reserved for officials or wealthy people, the rare exceptions being burials during Holy Week or at Christmas.

Other striking vehicles include a Studebaker and a 1976 Buick, both of which suggest a less formal style of funeral.

A close look at the exhibits also reveals many symbols linked to death, both in the hearses and on the employees' uniforms. For example, the Greek letters alpha and omega, which symbolize the beginning and the end. Also note the figure of an owl, a symbol of solitude, silence, and death, or that of Athena, the Greek goddess of wisdom, whom we are supposed to meet in the next world.

If you want to know more about the death industry, Barcelona's funerary services also run a coffin factory, which you can visit by special arrangement, although it is not normally open to the public.

DIPÒSIT DE LES AIGÜES

(19)

One of the best-kept architectural secrets in Barcelona

Pompeu Fabra University
Carrer de Ramón Trías Fargas, 39
93 542 1709
Monday–Friday 8am–1pm, Saturday 8am–2pm
Metro Ciutadella Vila Olímpica

The Dipòsit de les Aigües (Water Deposit) is one of the best-kept architectural secrets of the city. The building, inspired by the Mirabilis Roman baths, was constructed in 1880 by the architect Josep Fontserè. It was designed as a reservoir for water, hence the vaulted ceilings and brick walls resting on forty-eight pillars.

But over the years it has been used as a retirement home, a fire service warehouse, a film studio, an improvized hospital during the war, and finally, a university library.

In the 1970s, Pompeu Fabra University bought the building, thinking that it was an ideal opportunity to expand its facilities. Architects Lluís Clotet and Ignacio Paricio were commissioned to transform the space and adapt it to the needs of a library.

Apart from the effect of the million books stored here and the powerful architecture, the library has another distinctive feature.

Silence is of course the norm, but if you listen carefully, the roaring of lions and tigers can be heard through the huge windows. This is no illusion, the library is next door to Barcelona Zoo.

NEARBY

Tàpies' consultation room

In Pompeu Fabra University, a few metres from the library, is a very strange 'contemplation room.' In this lay chapel, there are no saints or gods to be worshipped, but simply two canvases: *Díptic de la campana* and *Serp i plat*, both works by Antoni Tàpies. This room, designed by the Catalan sculptor and painter, contains some twenty chairs fixed to the wall. The original idea was to create a space where visitors could come to terms with themselves, call upon a personal deity, or just admire two brilliant works by Tàpies in absolute silence. If you would like to visit this meditative space, just ask permission at reception.

THE KISS OF DEATH ㉑

One of the strangest tombs in the Poblenou cemetery

Cementerio de Poblenou – Carmen Amaya s/n
93 484 1780
Monday to Sunday 8am–6pm
El Santet: division 1, inner plot 4
Metro Poblenou

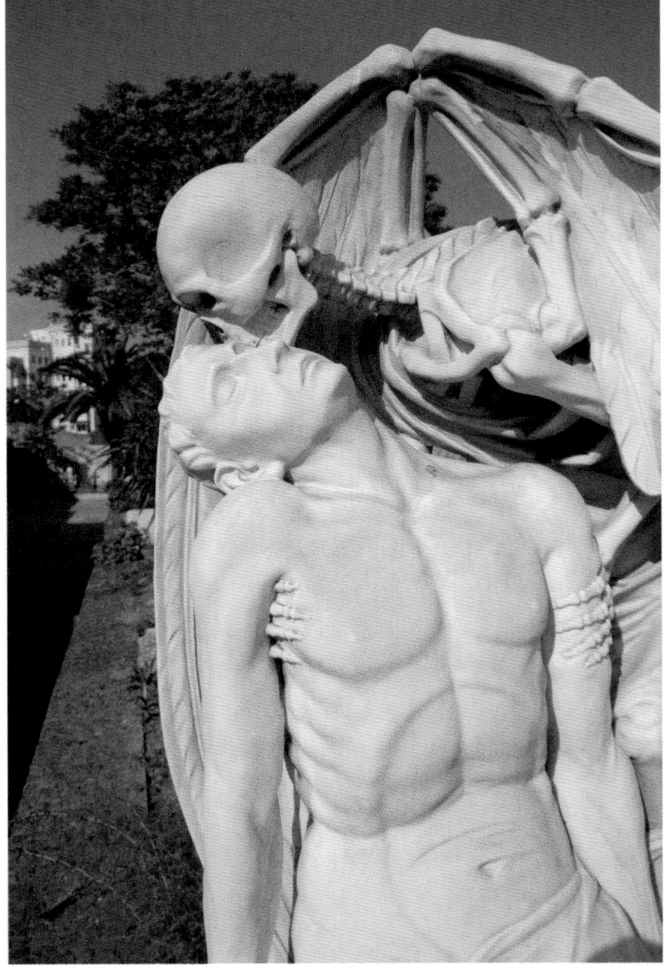

The Kiss of Death is one of the strangest tombs in the Poblenou cemetery. In this masterpiece by J. Barba, a winged death's head is simply kissing the forehead of the deceased. The marble sculpture is a tribute to a dead son. In 1991, it was one of the works most commented on in a Berlin exhibition on the theme of eroticism (!).

El Santet is another strange tomb, with an improvised altar carrying the most surrealist offerings to be seen in the cemetery, such as coffee caramels, cigarettes, and throat pastilles.

Francesc Canals Ambrós (Barcelona, 1879–899), known as 'El Santet,' was killed in an accident just before his twentieth birthday. Shortly afterwards, the rumour arose that El Santet granted people's prayers. From then on, the number of believers grew and grew, and his tomb is now always covered in flowers and other offerings.

Behind the walls of the Poblenou cemetery, over 5 metres high, lies a good part of the history of 19th-century Barcelona. The 'old cemetery,' as the locals call it, is embedded in a traditional neighbourhood that is beginning to give way to modern buildings. It lies almost opposite one of the beaches most popular with young people, Mar Bella.

The cemetery was opened in 1775 in an attempt to solve public sanitation problems. Although now within the urban area, it was originally some distance from the city, outside the walls.

The old cemetery brings together various architectural and aesthetic styles arranged in almost chronological order, and provides a wonderful opportunity to gain some understanding of the personalities and events of another age.

NEARBY

The stone that marks an ancient boundary (22)

Parc Carlos I

A symbolic stone in the Carlos I park, between Carrer de Marina and Carrer del Doctor Trueta, is in fact one of the boundary stones that used to mark the limits of the municipalities of Sant Martí and Barcelona. The inscription 'B i SM' engraved on the stone recalls its original function. The former village of Sant Martí de Provençals was annexed by Barcelona in 1897. Vast factories installed themselves in the district, earning it the nickname 'Catalonian Manchester.'

CHEEKY STUFFED PARROT IN POBLENOU LIQUOR STORE

(23)

A parrot that imitated the sound of the stationmaster's whistle

Licorera del Poblenou - Carrer Taulat, 91
93 225 26 66
Mon–Sat 9am–2pm & 5pm–9pm; Sun 9.30am–3pm
Metro Poblenou

At No. 91 Carrer Taulat, right in the old town centre of Poblenou, is an iconic liquor store whose doors have been open since 1932. What makes it special is not just the welcoming and dedicated way it's run by Júlia Cahuer, third generation in the business, or the display cabinets that make you feel like a gladiator in the arena, looking out at the hundreds of bottles arranged in the stands, but one small detail: a stuffed grey parrot who is now pretty much the neighbourhood mascot.

While still alive, the 'Lloro del 36' or 'No. 36 parrot' as it was known, was the thorn in the side of many a driver on tram lines 36 and 52, which stopped right in front of the store.

The wily creature, whose cage used to be hung outside so it could get a bit of sunshine and fresh air, managed to perfect an imitation of the stationmaster's whistle, creating traffic chaos as drivers rushed out of the nearby bars to get their vehicles moving without realizing it wasn't yet time.

Bewildered passengers would often lose their luggage in the mayhem while others simply missed their trams because they left early.

Finally, due to the amount of trouble the little parrot was causing, the liquor store owners were issued with a formal complaint requiring them to keep it shut up inside the shop.

And so it was that the parrot no longer caused havoc on the trams, and they went back to running as normal. However, dissatisfied with the prevailing social calm, the 'Lloro del 36' spent its days calling people drunkards, shouting 'torrat', a typical Catalan expression literally meaning 'toasted', often used to berate those who've had a drop too much.

Nowadays, as part of the local bestiary, Poblenou's 'Colla de Gegants' procession includes a figure dedicated to the 'Lloro del 36', wearing a tram-driver's cap and a whistle, and its stuffed body is still on display in the liquor store.

Bear one thing in mind: the norms regulating iconic establishments mean that you can't take photos inside, so if you want to see the parrot you'll have to be there.

TORRE DE LES AIGÜES DEL BESÒS

(24)

A tower that never served its purpose but is a wonderful viewpoint

A climb up to the top of the Torre de les Aigües
Plaça Ramon Calsina
Sat 12pm (tours in Catalan and Spanish; other languages on request)
Tours for groups of up to 15 people can be arranged; also night tours with cava
torredelesaigues.cat
Metro Selva de Mar

Built in 1882 by the architect Pere Falqués, the Tower of the Waters (Torre de les Aigües del Bèsos) is no secret in itself. However, what few people know is that once a week you can climb up its 311 steps and take in the extraordinary views over the city (by both day and night) and marvel at how Barcelona has evolved since the 1992 Olympics.

Despite the fact that it was never possible to get drinking water from it as intended (see below), the tower did finally have an industrial use, even if it never made the sort of profits that had been expected. However, it served as inspiration for the artists Josep Maria Subirachs and Ramon Calsina, after whom the square is named.

Its importance lies in the way it bears witness to the industrialisation of Catalonia and the efforts of the workers of the day. It is also part of a project aimed at recovering the symbols of industrial development. Over the years it has become a reference point for locals, a place for children to play and a silent witness to the transformation of the neighbourhood, where more buildings go up every day.

Suicide at the Torre de les Aigües – a monument to human error

At first it was thought that the tower would serve to extract drinking water, but the scheme did not take into account the fact that the proximity of the sea would lead to salt water filtering through. The project was a disaster and the entrepreneur who financed the works died soon after the analyses confirmed the salt levels in the water, making it unfit for human consumption. Although the cause of his death was not made public at the time, everything would seem to indicate that, crushed by the project's calamitous outcome, he threw himself off the top of the building.

THE THINKER OF POBLENOU

25

A theatre set designer's statue

Passatge d'Olivé, 17
Metro Glòries

On Passatge d'Olivé you'll find a reproduction of Rodin's *The Thinker* that has become one of the neighbourhood icons in this low-level housing area.

Poblenou, particularly the district now known as 22@ (Catalan *vint-i-dos arrova*), was once mainly made up of industrial businesses and workshops. At No. 3 Passatge d'Olivé i Maristany, in a building that has since disappeared, there used to be a workshop belonging to an artisan who made theatre set designs. For some reason he decided to make this copy of the famous sculpture and place it on top of the wall overlooking the street.

Over the years the reproduction started to catch the eyes of curious passers-by who would go over and take photographs of it. But the unstoppable force of real estate growth in the city made the existence of these small businesses in the middle of the city unviable. The workshop itself was abandoned and bricked up some years ago, but the thinker remains lost, as ever, in thought.

When plans emerged to demolish the building, the locals feared that the statue, which was now like part of the family, would be lost.

So residents at No. 17 offered to keep it on a temporary basis until they could decide what to do with it. The idea was evidently popular with the rest of the locals, given that not many would have had space to store it.

But what was meant to be temporary ended up becoming permanent, to the extent that now the Thinker of Poblenou has a new house where it can continue to cogitate from the top of the façade.

Perhaps to make the statue feel more at home, the hospitable family that took it in painted the handrail on the façade the same colour as the thinker, who waits, patiently and painstakingly restored, for new visitors. What few know is that this peculiar sculpture is made from porexpan (expanded polystyrene).

PARC DEL CENTRE DEL POBLENOU

(26)

One of the oddest parks in the city

10am–sunset (depending on hours of sunlight)
Metro Poblenou, Selva de Mar (L4)

Caught in the intersection between four streets (Bilbao, Marroc, Bac de Roda and Diagonal) you will find the beautiful Parc del Centre del Poblenou. Although it has more than 55,000 square metres of gardens, the park is little known or frequented by either tourists or locals. Yet it is, without doubt, one of the oddest parks in the city, where absolutely all the elements have some out-of-the-ordinary aspect: inorganically shaped benches; lighting hanging alongside vines; spherical lights in the ground which, on lighting up, are reminiscent of the night sky; strange little pinnacles that rise up towards the sky with vegetal shapes …

Located in the old industrial area of Poblenou and first opened in 2007, the park was designed by the Jean Nouvel architectural studio in collaboration with that of the Madrid architect Fermín Vázquez. The concept was similar to that of Gaudí: the natural garden elements are the essential axis around which the architecture itself revolves, so these

© Christine Zenino

elements cannot be understood without the built structures and vice versa.

This means that the park changes its appearance depending on the time of year. To generate a feeling of continuity between the different areas of the park, which is separated by Carrer Espronceda, there is one element that may be its most surprising part: almost half of the visible sky is covered by vegetation, which blooms in the spring, creating a unique blossom tunnel effect. The inside has rest areas, ping-pong tables, a space for pets and even an old factory-cum-museum, the Oliva-Artés Centre of the Museu d'Història de Barcelona (Barcelona History Museum: MUHBA).

The outside walls are covered by thick Mediterranean vegetation, which generates a feeling of nature beyond the park's actual borders. The fact that this is a large space, which is not often used by the locals, and that it is also an industrial area that has not really been developed, means this is the ideal location for getting away from all the hubbub of the city centre.

SOCIEDAD COLOMBÓFILA DE BARCELONA

27

The world of pigeons

Passatge del Taulat, 7
606 95 86 37
Federación Catalana de Colombicultura
Metro Poblenou

For over eighty years, the Barcelona pigeon-fanciers club and federation have been breeding pigeons.

The society, with its homing pigeons, and the federation, with its racing birds, are almost exclusively for men. They organize outdoor activities and meetings that revolve around the world of pigeons. Racing pigeons are by definition aggressive birds: nervous, resilient, and tireless. They are also courtship experts.

Homing pigeons, on the other hand, have very different traits. They are more docile, friendly, and always return to their lofts.

They also have a more athletic body shape. Their breeding and training is very different from that of racing pigeons as they develop an instinct for orientation rather than speed.

The skills of the two types of bird are tested in spring and summer.

Homing pigeons

Whether released at distances of 500 m or 100 km, and in certain cases, even over 1,000 km, the homing pigeon has the fantastic ability to always find its way back home. Although the reason for this exceptional skill is still unknown, some people attribute the pigeons' gift to the presence of tiny crystals in the brain. This trait was detected a long time ago, notably by Julius Caesar who used homing pigeons in his invasion of Gaul to send messages back to Rome and inform his followers of the campaign's progress.

On the other hand, make no mistake: there is no such thing as the pigeon you sometimes see in films, which is released to take a message somewhere and then returns. The pigeon is only (so to speak) capable of journeying homewards. This is why, in order to send a message to several different places, pigeons raised at each destination have to be taken out.

To carry several successive messages to the same place, the requisite number of pigeons would be needed ... There's nothing at all miraculous about this, and moving pigeons from one loft to another will make it difficult to pick up your messages ...

ALPHABETICAL INDEX

It was September 1995 and Thomas Jonglez was in Peshawar, the northern Pakistani city 20 kilometres from the tribal zone he was to visit a few days later. It occurred to him that he should record the hidden aspects of his native city, Paris, which he knew so well. During his seven-month trip back home from Beijing, the countries he crossed took in Tibet (entering clandestinely, hidden under blankets in an overnight bus), Iran and Kurdistan. He never took a plane but travelled by boat, train or bus, hitchhiking, cycling, on horseback or on foot, reaching Paris just in time to celebrate Christmas with the family.

On his return, he spent two fantastic years wandering the streets of the capital to gather material for his first 'secret guide', written with a friend. For the next seven years he worked in the steel industry until the passion for discovery overtook him. He launched Jonglez Publishing in 2003 and moved to Venice three years later.

In 2013, in search of new adventures, the family left Venice and spent six months travelling to Brazil, via North Korea, Micronesia, the Solomon Islands, Easter Island, Peru and Bolivia.

After seven years in Rio de Janeiro, he now lives in Berlin with his wife and three children.

Jonglez Publishing produces a range of titles in nine languages, released in 40 countries.

FROM THE SAME PUBLISHER

ATLAS

Atlas of geographical curiosities

PHOTO BOOKS

Abandoned America
Abandoned Asylums
Abandoned Australia
Abandoned churches – Unclaimed places of worship
Abandoned cinemas of the world
Abandoned France
Abandoned Germany
Abandoned Italy
Abandoned Japan
Abandoned Lebanon
Abandoned Spain
Abandoned USSR
After the Final Curtain – Vol. 1
After the Final Curtain – Vol. 2
Baikonur – Vestiges of the Soviet space programme
Forbidden Places – Vol. 1
Forbidden Places – Vol. 2
Forbidden Places – Vol. 3
Forgotten Heritage
Oblivion
Unusual wines
Venice deserted
Venice from the skies

'SECRET' GUIDES

Secret Amsterdam
Secret Bali – An unusual guide
Secret Bangkok
Secret Belfast
Secret Berlin
Secret Brighton – An unusual guide
Secret Brooklyn
Secret Brussels
Secret Buenos Aires
Secret Campania
Secret Cape Town
Secret Copenhagen
Secret Corsica
Secret Dublin – An unusual guide
Secret Edinburgh – An unusual guide
Secret Florence
Secret French Riviera
Secret Geneva
Secret Glasgow
Secret Granada
Secret Helsinki
Secret Istanbul
Secret Johannesburg
Secret Lisbon
Secret Liverpool – An unusual guide
Secret London – An unusual guide
Secret London – Unusual bars & restaurants
Secret Los Angeles – An unusual guide
Secret Madrid
Secret Mexico City
Secret Milan
Secret Montreal – An unusual guide
Secret Naples
Secret New Orleans
Secret New York – An unusual guide
Secret New York – Curious activities
Secret New York: Hidden bars & restaurants
Secret Paris
Secret Prague
Secret Provence
Secret Rio
Secret Rome
Secret Seville
Secret Singapore
Secret Sussex – An unusual guide
Secret Tokyo
Secret Tuscany
Secret Venice
Secret Vienna
Secret Washington D.C.
Secret York – An unusual guide

'SOUL OF' GUIDES

Soul of Amsterdam – A guide to the 30 best experiences
Soul of Athens – A guide to 30 exceptional experiences
Soul of Barcelona – A guide to 30 exceptional experiences
Soul of Berlin – A guide to the 30 best experiences
Soul of Kyoto – A guide to 30 exceptional experiences
Soul of Lisbon – A guide to 30 exceptional experiences
Soul of Los Angeles – A guide to 30 exceptional experiences
Soul of Marrakesh – A guide to 30 exceptional experiences
Soul of New York – A guide to 30 exceptional experiences
Soul of Rome – A guide to 30 exceptional experiences
Soul of Tokyo – A guide to 30 exceptional experiences
Soul of Venice – A guide to 30 exceptional experiences

Follow us on Facebook, Instagram and Twitter

ACKNOWLEDGEMENTS
Vitor Adrião, María Antón, Alexandra Barba, Josep Baucells, José Bauer, Manuel Bauer, Fiorella Battistini, Elena Bort, Cristina Garrido Buxeda, Jose Antonio Capin, Lluís Casamitjana, Melissa Chiarella, Mònica Coluchon, Yaki Creiger, Trinidad Delor, Olivia Denoyelle, Alejandra Devéscovi, Giselle Etcheverry, María Galaxia, Nabila Giha, Nicolás Giha, Camila González, Francesca Goytisolo, Carlos Granés, Fietta Jarque, Helena Liñan, María del Mar López, José Roman Moral Maeso, Ishka Michocka, Eva Morla, Marc Permanyer, José Muñoz Reales, Marianella Muro, Mutual de Conductors, Sarah Parot, José Pérez Freijo, Silvia Pérez López, Olga Perucho, Iu Pino, Carlos Ramírez, Mali Ramírez, Rufina Redondo, Isabella Reich, Lola Repiso, Jaime Reula, Natasha Rigas, Olga Sala, Craig Sanders, Vicenta Sebastián, Fernando Sierra, Jorge Soto, Meritxell Tellez, Morgana Vargas Llosa, Juan Miguel Varón, Manuel Vázquez, Manuel Villate, Hotel Omm, Hotel La Florida.

PHOTOS CREDITS
Jaime Reula: Statue of the black Madonna of Montserrat - Flaming heart sculpture - Streetlamps in Plaça del Rei - Portrait of Fructuós Canonge - *A room where it always rains* sculpture - *The temptation of man* sculpture - Josep Guardiola's initials - Monument to Ferrer i Guàrdia - Jardín de Jaume Viçens i Vives - *L'Empordà. Oda nova a Barcelona* - Pavelló de la Repùblica - Plaque commemorating the guerrilla Facerías
Carlos Mesa: Face of Gaudí - Correos, the phantom metro station - Masonic symbols at Sant Agustí monastery - FC Barcelona shield
Jacques Garance: Club Ateneu Barcelonés - Lion of St Mark - Traces of shrapnel from the civil war - Saint Lucy's yardstick - Streets in the Barri Gòtic named after guilds - Symbols of Saint Stephen's guild - Angel of Plaça de l'Ángel - Remains of a Roman temple - Traces of prostitutes - Wheel of the innocents - Sagrada Familia labyrinth - Cyclist of Casa Macaya - La Primitiva, bar & ornithological society - Sociedad colombófila de Barcelona
Ishka Michocka: Friends of the Railway Association - Hand of Barceloneta - Advertisement for the Anís del Mono - Four faces of the Bosque cinema - Horta washerwomen - Museu de Carrosses Fúnebres
Rocio Sierra: Hare Krishna temple - Capella de Sant Cristòfor del Regomir - *En la prensa de aquel día...* - Anatomy lecture hall - *El Torn dels orfes* - Arús public library - Garden of Torre de las Aguas - Museu del perfum - Barcelona seminary's museum of geology - School of San Miguel del Sagrado Corazón - Comte d'Urgell traffic lights - Agrupació Astronòmica de Barcelona (ASTER) - Monument to the metre at Montjuïc castle - Refugi 307 - Other air-raid shelters - Clínica Barraquer - Museum of antique automats - Kagyu Samye Dzong - Turó de la Rovira - Carrer de Sòcrates bomb - Monument to the metre - *The Kiss of Death* - Torre de les Aigües del Besòs
VMA: Montjuïc cemetery - Sculptures at Casa de la Lactancia: DR - Dipòsit de les Aigües: UPF
Maya Riera Camps: Stone trees in Casa Antónia Burés - Tomb of Pere Vintró Sagristà - Arús public library - Dark *panots* on Passeig de Gràcia - Stone plaque for the miracles of Josep Oriol

Cartography: **Cyrille Suss** - Layout: **Emmanuelle Willard Toulemonde** - Translation: **Caroline Lawrence and Dan Whitcombe** - Editing: **Jana Gough** - Proofreading: **Kimberly Bess**- Publishing: **Clémence Mathé**

Registration of copyright: May 2023 – Edition: 03
ISBN: 978-2-36195-308-9
Printed in Bulgaria by Multiprint